Day Hikes in the Santa Fe Area

Founded in 1892, the Sierra Club works in the United States and other countries to restore the quality of the natural environment and to maintain the integrity of ecosystems. Educating the public to understand and support these objectives is a basic part of the Club's program. All are invited to participate in its activities, which include programs to "...study, explore, and enjoy wildlands."

From _Sierra_: The Sierra Club Bulletin

DAY HIKES
IN THE
SANTA FE AREA
Third Edition

New and Enlarged

By The Santa Fe Group
Of The Sierra Club

TABLE OF CONTENTS

ACKNOWLEDGMENTS

So many people have helped with the third edition of this book that it is impossible to give formal recognition to all of them. However, some people have contributed so much time, thought and energy to this project that they deserve special thanks.

First of all, thanks are due to the authors of the individual hikes for sharing their knowledge and love of the outdoors and for accepting with good humor and understanding the revisions made by the editors.

Betsy Fuller was the driving force behind the third edition of this book. She coordinated the efforts of all the contributors and provided the momentum needed to bring this labor of love to a happy conclusion.

Bill Chudd and Norbert Sperlich deserve special recognition for their imagination, commitment and perseverance in putting the final product together. They, along with Betsy, as editors-in-chief, made the final decisions on content and form and spent countless hours editing, brainstorming and proof-reading.

Special thanks go to Linda Zwick. She spent numerous lunch hours patiently and cheerfully typing and retyping the hikes as they came to her from the editors. Her expertise on the word processor is awesome. Many grateful thanks are also due to her employers, White, Koch, Kelly & McCarthy, who generously allowed the use of their word processor and copying machine.

For the appearance of the final product, we are indebted to Wes Horner for the sketch maps, to Robin Bond for her line drawings and to Dorothy Grossman for the cover design.

Many thanks go to Ingrid Vollnhofer, John Muchmore, and Art Judd who have shared their considerable experience and knowledge of the area. Ann Young first picked up the idea of a trail guide for the Santa Fe area and provided the spark that produced the first two editions. Ken Adam and Wes Horner deserve many thanks for handling the printing arrangements.

Every hike in this book has been test-hiked by people unfamiliar with the trails. Many thanks go to these "scouts" who checked out the hikes and gave suggestions to update and improve the hiking instructions and driving directions. They are: Lë Adams, Ann Bancroft, Myles Brown, David Clark, E. J. Evangelos, Anna Heiniger, John Jasper, Allison Leon, Don Lowrie, Dan Mitchem, John Muchmore, Ed Okun, Betsy Reed, Norbert Sperlich, Ingrid Vollnhofer, and Bill and Linda Zwick.

INTRODUCTION

by
Betsy Fuller

The area around Santa Fe contains a wealth
of varied hikes perhaps unequaled by any
other place in the state. Access to the
13,000 foot peaks of the Sangre de Cristo
Mountains is within an hour's drive of the
main plaza. Winter walks at elevations of
less than 6,000 feet are within easy reach
when the mountains are too deep in snow to
be walked. There are three nationally desig-
nated wilderness areas within an hour and a
half's drive and the Santa Fe National
Forest contains over a million and a half
acres of federal land. Within an hour's
drive of Santa Fe you can find five of the
seven life zones.

For several years the Santa Fe Group of the
Sierra Club has felt the need for some kind
of guide to this wealth of wilderness and
this volume describes some of the typical
walks that are so close. We have included
walks that are classed as easy as well as
more difficult ones, and we have tried to
give fair representation to the many varied
types of terrain that are within easy
driving distance of Santa Fe.

There are excellent guides already in print
describing trails in Bandelier National
Monument and in the Sandia Mountains. Because of these, we have limited the number
of hikes described in those two areas to one

or two representative ones. If those areas are the ones that appeal to you for future exploration, be sure to refer to these publications. They are listed in the "Suggested Reading" section at the back of the book.

Two printings of the first edition of this book and a large printing of the second edition have been sold out. Rather than reprinting the second edition, the editors have decided that the time had come for a completely revised third edition. There are thirteen new hikes in this edition; three hikes from the earlier editions have been omitted.

The money earned from the sales of the book has been used in a variety of environmental campaigns including efforts to save old timber stands from logging, to save pristine wilderness areas from mining operations, to prevent toxic ash from being released into the atmosphere and to have nearby waterways declared wild and scenic rivers.

HOW TO USE THIS BOOK

The 37 hikes in this book are arranged according to geographical area. Twenty-four hikes will take you to the Sangre de Cristo Mountains, foothills included. There are three hikes to the volcanoes of the Caja del Rio, and six hikes to the Pajarito Plateau and the Jemez Mountains west of the Rio Grande. The last four hikes are each in a different geographic area. The map on page xx shows the approximate location of the hikes and the chart on pages xxi and xxii tells you the difficulty of a hike and the appropriate season.

The hikes are graded as "easy," "moderate," and "strenuous," but these terms are extremely loose and may mean different things to different hikers. It would probably be wise for a hiker new to the area to attempt one of the shorter hikes first to see how his rating compares with the editors'. In general we call a hike easy if it is under six miles in length and involves relatively little elevation change. A moderate hike is usually between six and ten miles, involves more uphill climbing and may be over less well maintained trails. A strenuous hike is over ten miles in length, usually involves substantial changes in elevation, is often at high elevations and sometimes is over very rough trails.

Weather conditions in the area around Santa Fe vary widely from day to day and from season to season. If you have any doubt about the advisabilty of taking a hike, check with the Highway Department for road conditions and with the Santa Fe National Forest office for trail conditions.

Before you start on the hike, read through the preliminary material and the hiking directions to be sure that it's the kind of outing you have in mind. You might find from a preliminary reading that you'll want to take a camera or a wildflower field guide or a pair of binoculars for birding.

The sketch maps at the beginning of each chapter are not meant to be used as trail guides, but only to give a general idea of the length, direction and "shape" of the walk. We urge you to purchase the U.S. Geological Survey topographical map or maps that cover the area of the hike in which you are interested. The topographical maps needed are listed at the beginning of each

hike and are available at most sporting
goods stores in Santa Fe or from the U.S.
Geological Survey, Federal Center, Denver,
Colorado 80225. If you're not familiar with
these maps, spend some time studying them so
that you'll recognize what the contour lines
mean, which way is uphill or downhill, what
the scale is and what the symbols mean.
Compare it with the trail description and
the sketch map in the book. It might be a
good idea to pencil in on the topo map the
route you'll be following. Even these maps
occasionally contain errors and omissions.
With experience, you'll probably learn to
use not only the maps and the trail descriptions, but also your own intuition and
outdoor skills to find your way in the
wilderness.

In addition to the topo map, it will be
helpful to have a New Mexico road map and
also maps of the Santa Fe National Forest
and the Carson National Forest where most of
these hikes are located. These maps are
available at the Santa Fe National Forest
Office, Piñon Building, 1220 St. Francis
Drive, Santa Fe, New Mexico. If you're
hiking in the Sangre de Cristo Mountains a
map called "Pecos Wilderness" put out by the
Santa Fe National Forest is helpful and is
available at the address above.

You should take along a simple compass and a
pencil and small memo pad. Usually the
directions and turns on the trails are given
as "left" or "right," but in several walks
it is necessary to know the compass reading. The pencil and pad will be helpful to
have so that you can make notes of starting
times and odometer readings and can keep a
record of how long it takes you to cover
distances compared with the times given in
the book.

Every effort has been made to make the directions, both driving and hiking, easy to understand and accurate. However, this book should not be considered to be a step-by-step, do-it-yourself hiking book for beginners. Because of changes in the routes of trails, vandalism of signs, destruction of man-made landmarks, as well as the possibility of human error, accuracy of every detail cannot be guaranteed. Mileages given are necessarily inexact. If you haven't hiked in the mountains or remote areas before, don't start out alone with this guide as your only companion. Find a more experienced hiker to accompany you or join one of the Sierra Club outings which are scheduled every weekend and which are led by experienced hikers who are willing to share their knowledge with you. More information on these weekly hikes can be obtained by calling the Sierra Club office in Santa Fe.

One final word; wilderness is destructible, so when you are in it, respect it, love it and take care of it. Stay on the trails and don't take shortcuts. Pack out your trash to the last gum wrapper; even pack out somebody else's trash. Be careful with matches. Admire the flowers and rocks, but leave them there for the next passerby to admire too. And remember that you are only visiting where other animals live, so treat them and their environment with the respect you'd like to receive where you live.

Happy hiking!

SAFETY TIPS FOR HIKERS

by
Herb Kincey
St. John's College Search and Rescue Team

Certain safety procedures should be followed
by anyone going into wild country. Failure
to observe safety rules can lead to acci-
dents and sometimes death. Chances of
becoming a statistic in the records of some
search and rescue team will be greatly re-
duced by following these safety rules.

DO NOT GO ALONE: Unless you are experienced
and prefer solitude, a party of at least
four persons is recommended. Then if one
person is injured, one can remain with the
victim while the other two go for help. Try
never to leave an injured hiker alone.

PLAN YOUR ROUTE CAREFULLY: Know the escape
routes. Plan a route ahead of time using
U.S. Geological Survey and U.S. Forest
Service maps. When traveling on foot allow
about one hour for each two miles covered
plus an additional hour for each 1000 feet
of altitude gained. At all times know where
you are on the map and the best way out to
civilization.

GET WEATHER REPORTS AND BE PREPARED FOR
EMERGENCIES: Fast moving frontal systems
can bring sudden and violent changes in New
Mexico weather, especially during winter.
Try to obtain an extended weather forecast
before setting out. Although even the

highest peaks in New Mexico are considered "walkups" from a technical standpoint during summer months, nevertheless, they are above timberline and they are remote. On long hikes or scrambles above timberline the safe policy is to start for the summit at dawn and turn back about noon, the time when summer storms begin to form.

CHECK WITH AUTHORITIES: Most of the New Mexico high country lies within National Forests. Forest rangers know their districts and can offer valuable advice on trails, campsites and potential problems. Many desert lands are administered by the Bureau of Land Management (BLM) whose officials will be glad to help. The New Mexico Department of Game and Fish will be glad to make recommendations about where to hike during hunting seasons. A booklet from this department describes the areas open to hunters along with season dates. This is a useful publication for individuals wishing to avoid hunting areas. Bright clothing is appropriate from a safety standpoint during big game hunting season.

GO PROPERLY EQUIPPED: As a rule the most serious dangers in the wilderness are WIND, COLD and WETNESS. Even during July it sometimes snows on the higher peaks, and hard summer rains occur almost daily through the mountain ranges. It is quite possible to die from "exposure," technically hypothermia, at any time of the year, especially above timberline (about 11,800 feet). Having warm clothing, even during the summer, is very important. A shirt, sweater, socks, mittens and cap (all of wool or polypropylene) should always be carried. Even when wet, wool is warm against the skin. For protection against wind and wetness carry a weatherproof outer parka or poncho.

One of the first signs of hypothermia is shivering. This may be followed by difficulty walking and speaking, confusion, drowsiness and even coma. Steps should be taken to restore and maintain body temperature as soon as signs of hypothermia are noticed. These steps may include locating shelter from the elements, use of warm clothing or blankets if available, replacing cold wet clothing, providing warm, non-alcoholic drinks and body-to-body transfer of heat. If symptoms intensify medical help should be obtained as soon as possible.

Always carry these items with you when going into the back country: map, compass, flashlight, sunglasses, waterproof matches, whistle, pocket knife, candle, protective clothing, minimum first aid, extra food and water. Water is very scarce in some areas. Carry plenty, at least a quart per person. Water purification tablets are recommended if you drink water from streams or lakes. Giardia is now a common problem in most New Mexico wilderness areas.

ALLOW TIME FOR ACCLIMATIZATION: Persons going into high mountains from low altitudes should beware of trying to climb any of the major peaks until they have had a few days to acclimatize. Many people who go too high too fast suffer "mountain sickness." The symptoms are vomiting, diarrhea, and the feeling of being very ill. Pulmonary edema, a major medical emergency, also can occur above the 8000 foot level. The symptoms include extreme fatigue or collapse, shortness of breath, a racking cough, bubbling noises in the chest and bloody sputum. Unless transported to a much lower altitude immediately the victim may die within a matter of hours. If available, administer oxygen until reaching a hospital.

Several other proceaures may help prevent the "mountain miseries": arrive in good physical condition, get plenty of rest and sleep and avoid alcohol and smoking.

LEAVE INFORMATION WITH RELATIVES OR FRIENDS: An itinerary of your trip, along with the names and addresses of each member, description and license numbers of vehicles used, and expected time of return should be left with a reliable person. Once under way, stick to your planned route and schedule. Any time a group is seriously overdue or an accident has occurred, the New Mexico State Police should be called in order to obtain assistance.

LEARN THE LIMITATIONS OF EACH MEMBER: Assess the strengths and weaknesses of each member of the party. Do not try anything beyond the ability of the weakest hiker. Set the pace to that of the slowest hiker. Be willing to turn back when conditions warrant doing so.

KEEP THE PARTY TOGETHER: Individual members of a group should not be allowed to fall behind the main party or go ahead of it. Many wilderness fatalities have resulted from disregarding this rule. If the group is large, select one person to set the pace, another to bring up the rear. If hiking in the dark for some reason, assign each hiker a number and count off periodically.

WATCH FOR FLASH FLOODS: Most New Mexico streams are shallow and present few fording problems. However, flash floods occur in the steep arid canyons and arroyos around the perimeter of the mountains and even in

desert areas. Be especially careful in
these hazardous areas and do not camp in or
leave vehicles parked there.

BEWARE OF LOOSE ROCK: In some places loose
rock can be a serious hazard. Keep your
group bunched together when going up or down
this type of terrain. Never roll rocks down
a mountainside. Another party may be below
you.

GET OFF EXPOSED RIDGES DURING STORMS:
Summer storms move in fast and are accom-
panied by rain or hail, high winds, low
visibility and lightning. Try not to allow
your group to be caught on a peak or exposed
ridge. If you are unable to get down in a
lightning storm, have the group spread out
about 30 feet between each person. Stay
away from lone trees or rocks. Avoid
shallow caves or depressions, for ground
currents may jump from the edge to your
body. Insulate yourself from the ground if
possible (pack, rope, clothing) and squat
down, allowing only your two feet to touch
the ground or the improvised insulation
materials. Do not lie down.

EMERGENCY SIGNALS: The following signals
are considered standard by many search and
rescue groups.

DISTRESS - 3 evenly spaced signals given
within 30 seconds. Repeat as required.

ACKNOWLEDGMENT - 2 signals given in quick
succession.

RETURN TO CAMP - 4 evenly spaced signals
given within 30 seconds. Repeat as
required.

BACKGROUND OF SIERRA CLUB OUTINGS

by
Kenneth D. Adam

In 1892 a group of concerned and dedicated men met in an office in San Francisco to form an organization of those interested in mountain travel and exploration. The first president was John Muir, and there were 182 charter members. It was decided to call this organization the Sierra Club, and to include in its purposes the publication of authentic information about the mountains, and enlist the support and cooperation of the people and government in preserving the forests and natural features of the Sierra Nevada. It almost immediately took the lead in the successful battle to preserve Yosemite Valley and its high country as a National Park.

The club held its first outing in 1901. Members in the San Francisco Bay area started a program of local walks in 1904. Lovers of the outdoors in other areas soon became interested, so the Angeles Chapter was formed in Los Angeles in 1911. The first chapter outside of California was organized on the East Coast in 1950, known as the Atlantic Chapter.

The Rio Grande Chapter came into being in 1963 with 52 members, and initially included not only New Mexico, but all of Texas and the eastern part of Arizona. Almost immediately most of Texas and the entire state of Arizona formed their own chapters, leaving the Rio Grande Chapter with its present boundaries including the state of New Mexico and the El Paso area of Texas. In the early 1970's the Santa Fe Group of the Rio Grande Chapter was formed, and soon had an active outings and local walks program.

Almost every week visitors to Santa Fe, as well as newly arrived residents take advantage of the local Sierra Club hikes. They ask, "Are there other exciting places to walk in the area? How can we find them?" This book is an attempt to satisfy the needs of those who like to hike on their own, but are frustrated by lack of information about how to reach a trailhead, or what to expect when they do.

Map Legend

- - - - - trail

· · · · · · way (no trail)

⹀⹀⹀⹀⹀⹀ dirt road

⌇⌇⌇⌇ paved road

⌇⌇⌇⌇⌇ mesa edge

✕ saddle; low point is between curved lines

· — · — intermittent stream

⟩— permanent stream

NORTH ⟩ direction of true North. magnetic North is about 12° East of true North

---

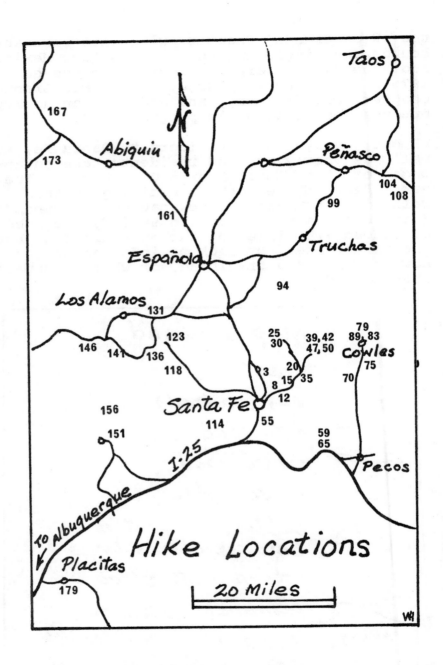

The numbers on this map are the page numbers
of the hike descriptions.

CHART OF HIKES

Difficulty: <u>E</u>=Easy, <u>M</u>=Moderate, <u>S</u>=Strenuous

Season: Time of year when hike is most suitable is indicated by a bar.

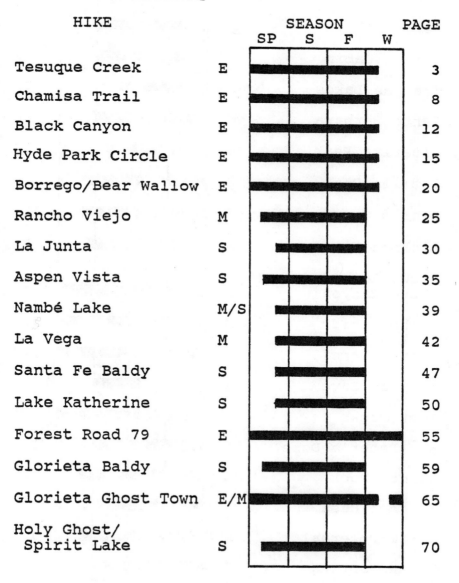

HIKE		SEASON				PAGE
		SP	S	F	W	
Tesuque Creek	E					3
Chamisa Trail	E					8
Black Canyon	E					12
Hyde Park Circle	E					15
Borrego/Bear Wallow	E					20
Rancho Viejo	M					25
La Junta	S					30
Aspen Vista	S					35
Nambé Lake	M/S					39
La Vega	M					42
Santa Fe Baldy	S					47
Lake Katherine	S					50
Forest Road 79	E					55
Glorieta Baldy	S					59
Glorieta Ghost Town	E/M					65
Holy Ghost/ Spirit Lake	S					70

HIKE		SP	S	F	W	PAGE
Beatty's Cabin	S		█	█		75
Dockwiller Trail	M		█	█		79
Stewart Lake	S		█	█		83
Pecos Baldy	S		█	█		89
Brazos Cabin	S		█	█		94
Trampas Lakes	S		█			99
Santa Barbara	M/S	█	█	█		104
Jicarita Peak	S		█	█		108
Tetilla Peak	E	█		█	█	114
Diablo Canyon	E	█	█	█	█	118
Buckman Mesa	M	█	█	█		123
Otowi Ruins/ Bayo Canyon	M	█		█	█	131
Ancho Rapids	M	█	█		█	136
Stone Lions	S	█	█	█	▪	141
Painted Cave	S	█	█	█		146
Tent Rocks	E	█	█	█	▪	151
St. Peter's Dome	S	█	█	█		156
Window Rock	M	█	█	█	▪	161
Kitchen Mesa	E/M	█	█	█	▪	167
Cerro Pedernal	M/S	█	█	█		173
Tunnel Spring	S	█	█	█		179

Day Hikes in the Santa Fe Area

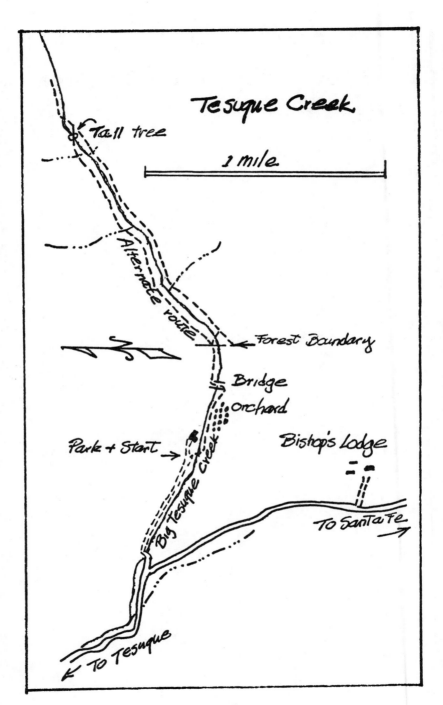

Tesuque Creek

1 mile

Tall tree

Alternate route

Forest Boundary

Bridge

Orchard

Park + Start

Big Tesuque Creek

Bishop's Lodge

To Santa Fe

To Tesuque

TESUQUE CREEK

by
Katie Parker

U.S. GEOLOGICAL SURVEY MAP REQUIRED: Santa Fe - 7.5 minute series.

SALIENT FEATURES: The trail is an interesting combination of ponderosa pine, piñon/juniper, and riparian woodlands. A flowing stream is this trail's most important feature.

RATING: Easy.

ROUND TRIP HIKING DISTANCE: 3 miles.

APPROXIMATE HIKING TIME: A very leisurely 2 hours.

ALTITUDE RANGE: Highest point, 7600 feet; lowest point, 7100 feet; total vertical ascent, 500 feet.

SEASONAL CONSIDERATIONS: At time of spring runoff, the stream rises above the logs and stones used to cross it and you must make your own log bridges or stepping stones, or else wade across the stream. The trail is passable during all but the snowiest months. You should be prepared for snow on the south side of the stream during the winter months.

ROUND TRIP DRIVING: 8.2 miles - about half an hour.

DRIVING DIRECTIONS: From the plaza drive north on Washington Avenue (which after about 4 blocks becomes Bishop's Lodge Road, Highway 590). In 3.5 miles, you will pass the entrance to Bishop's Lodge and almost exactly 1 mile beyond this entrance the paved road takes a sharp right angle turn to the left. Tesuque Creek is directly in front of you, as well as a sign with an arrow pointing to the left. Don't take this left turn. Take the dirt road to the right, County Road 72A. Drive 1/2 mile to the end of the public road where there is a rock pillar and three five-foot tall wooden posts. Do not park in front of the posts. Turn around here and park along the south side of the road where you won't be blocking traffic or driveways. The first part of this trail is an easement over private land and if the parking privilege is abused access here could be closed.

HIKING INSTRUCTIONS: The trail begins immediately beyond the five foot wooden posts. Stay on the trail to avoid encroaching on private land. You will immediately cross Big Tesuque Creek over a little wooden footbridge. The trail follows the river upstream. You will walk past an old abandoned vineyard and orchard on your right. After about 10 minutes you come out onto a dirt road. Go left over the car bridge and then turn right up the river. The trail follows the fence line. Look for woodpeckers in the cottonwood trees along the river bottom here.

In another 8 to 10 minutes, you will go through a Forest Service gate to enter the Santa Fe National Forest. Keep to the right as the trail forks soon after the gate. (You will return on the left fork.) Trail #254 crosses the stream to the south side.

About 25 feet after the stream crossing, the trail splits. Take the left trail fork. About 10 to 15 minutes later you will come to a rubble covered hill. Stay on the main trail here. About halfway up the rubble covered hill, the trail splits again. Bear left, following up the river. You are now in a lovely forest of ponderosa pines and most of the time will be 20 to 50 feet above the river. When you've been walking about 30 to 40 minutes, you'll note a very steep drop-off on your left. You can see the river directly below. Very soon you will come to another river crossing.

This is the turn-around point of this hike. Don't cross the river here. Turn around and go back down the trail about 35 yards/paces and you will see a very large ponderosa pine on the river side of the main trail. On the other side of the trail you'll notice a small wash coming down the hill. Now you should see your return trail going down the slope, under the big ponderosa pine and across the river. (There is no marker at this junction, so if you can't find it, return to the car the way you came.)

If you do find it, you will be going down-stream on the north side of the canyon. Notice how markedly different the vegeta-tion, soil and temperature are from the south side which you just walked up. Looking to your left across the Big Tesuque creek you can sometimes see the trail on the south side or hear other hikers on that trail.

The trail comes slowly down to the stream. It intersects Trail #254 (which you walked up) at the first stream crossing inside the National Forest Boundary. From here on you are reversing your steps. Go down the trail, through the Forest Service Gate, walk down along the north side of the creek until you again cross the big wooden bridge. Remember that your trail is just to the right beyond the wooden bridge. Walk downstream past the orchard and vineyard and then over the little wooden footbridge to your car.

N.B. You may not be ready to turn around at the second stream crossing. If so, continue on up the river as long as you want. This is a lovely extension over a well defined trail, but be warned, there are many stream crossings and you may come back with wet feet.

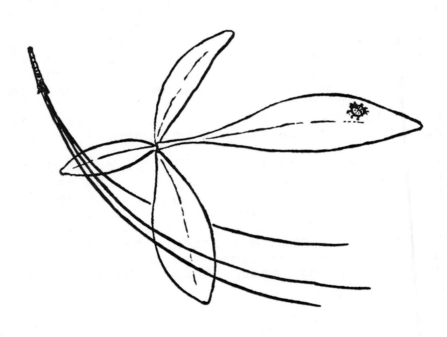

Chamisa Trail

1 mile

CHAMISA TRAIL

by
Bill Stone

U.S. GEOLOGICAL SURVEY MAPS REQUIRED: McClure Reservoir and Aspen Basin - 7.5 minute series. Much of the trail has been re-routed and parts of it are no longer as shown on these maps.

SALIENT FEATURES: A well-defined mountain trail through evergreen forest. A beautiful grassy meadow beside Big Tesuque Creek at the far point of the hike. Many wildflowers and birds in season. Close to Santa Fe.

RATING: Easy.

ROUND TRIP HIKING DISTANCE: 4.75 miles.

APPROXIMATE HIKING TIME: 2.5 to 3 hours.

ALTITUDE RANGE: Highest point, 8500 feet; lowest point, 7800 feet; total vertical ascent, 1240 feet.

SEASONAL CONSIDERATIONS: May be snowed-in and icy in midwinter.

ROUND TRIP DRIVING: 12 miles - approximately 30 minutes.

DRIVING DIRECTIONS: Leaving the main plaza, drive north on Washington Avenue 6 blocks and turn right on Artist Road. There is a sign here pointing to Hyde State Park and the Ski Basin. Measure your mileage from here. Artist Road becomes State Road 475 and you will see occasional green mileage markers as you continue uphill. Drive 5.6 miles to where there is a wide canyon on the north (left) side of the road. Park in the off-road parking spaces on either side of the road. The trail starts uphill near the road on the north side. There is a US Forest Service sign saying "Trail 183 - Big Tesuque 2 1/4." This is the Chamisa Trail.

HIKING INSTRUCTIONS: The trail goes due east for a few hundred feet and climbs sharply. It then turns due north. It is deeply forested, with piñon, two species of juniper, and ponderosa pine at the start. There are many switchbacks, and as you climb higher there are views of the canyon and the Hyde Park Road. Gambel oak and Douglas fir now appear. White (limber) pine and white fir appear at higher elevations. The trail is narrow, and at some places proceeds along a steep dugway, with little room to pass another person. The footing here is loose and sandy. After you have walked a mile and a quarter and climbed 700 feet, you will come to the crest of the trail (altitude 8500 feet). A trail coming up the canyon from the left meets #183 here. This is a good place for a break.

The trail now goes downhill. It turns sharply southeast, to your right as you approach, then, after a few hundred feet, toward northeast (left), and continues in a northerly direction for the rest of the hike. It proceeds down a dry stream bed (very wet in spring). The footing is rocky in places. Aspen is found here as well as the trees mentioned above. After one mile you come to a small grassy meadow. Continue about a quarter of a mile and you will see

two posts driven into the ground. This is
the junction with the Winsor Trail (#254).
The Chamisa Trail ends here. There is a
grassy meadow northeast (upstream) of the
junction, and the Big Tesuque Creek is on
its western border. The meadow is a beautiful, quiet spot and a good place to have
your lunch. There is a large granite
boulder in the middle of the meadow. The
altitude is 7960 feet. This is the furthest
point of the hike.

Return the way you came. Be sure to get
back on the same trail (Chamisa), by turning
left (south) at the two posts. The Chamisa
Trail is level at this point. The Winsor
Trail follows the Big Tesuque downstream.
The 540 foot climb back to the saddle is
moderate in most places, but very steep in
two. On reaching the saddle again (8500
feet) the trail divides. Take the trail to
the left, which is level here. This is the
trail you came up on. The other trail goes
down into the canyon and enters private
property. Proceed to the trailhead.

Many wildflowers and plants may be seen.
Among the predominant ones are Oregon grape,
yucca, scarlet gilia, red penstemon, lupine
(slopes near the crest are covered with its
blooms in the late spring), and many Composi-
tae. In addition, you may see mullein,
yellow evening primrose, yarrow, wild iris,
salsify , and coneflower in the meadows.

I have seen 42 species of birds along the
Chamisa Trail. Among them are hawks,
hummingbirds, woodpeckers, flycatchers,
swallows, jays, ravens, nuthatches, chicka-
dees, thrushes, warblers, vireos, and the
sparrow types.

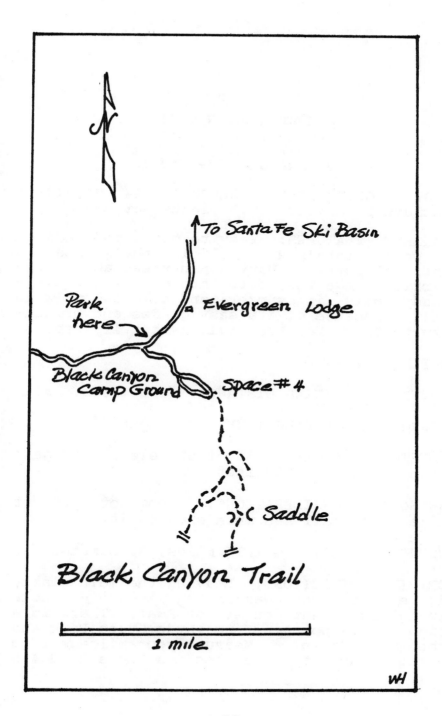

N

To Santa Fe Ski Basin

Park here →

Evergreen Lodge

Black Canyon Camp Ground

Space # 4

Saddle

Black Canyon Trail

1 mile

WH

BLACK CANYON TRAIL

by
Linda and Bill Zwick

U.S. GEOLOGICAL SURVEY MAP REQUIRED: McClure Reservoir - 7.5 minute series.

SALIENT FEATURES: Easy to moderate grade on a well-maintained trail in the Santa Fe National Forest. Many aspen trees and strawberries edge the route through the pines. A shady walk in summer and colorful walk in fall. Because of its easy grades and proximity to Santa Fe, the trail is heavily used.

RATING: Easy.

ROUND TRIP HIKING DISTANCE: Two miles.

APPROXIMATE HIKING TIME: One hour.

ALTITUDE RANGE: 500-foot elevation gain from 8,300 to 8,800 feet.

SEASONAL CONSIDERATIONS: Do not attempt hike when trail has much snow on it.

ROUND TRIP DRIVING: 15 miles; 30 minutes.

DRIVING DIRECTIONS: Leaving the main plaza, drive north on Washington Avenue 6 blocks and turn right on Artist Road. There is a sign here pointing to Hyde State Park and the Ski Basin. Measure your mileage from here. Artist Road becomes State Road 475 and you will see occasional green mileage markers as you continue uphill. Drive 7 miles to the Black Canyon Campground and park on your right outside the campground entrance along the rail fence as indicated by the parking signs. There is no fee for cars parked outside.

HIKING INSTRUCTIONS: Begin walk by following the paved road through Black Canyon Campground, being considerate of the paying campers by keeping your dog leashed and by staying on the road. Follow the road uphill until you reach Space 4, just beyond which the graveled trail begins. Approximately one-half mile from the beginning of the trail, the trail forks. Stay to the left, as the fork to the right leads to a watershed area closed to public access. The trail traverses to the saddle of the ridge along which beautiful views of the area attract your attention. Beyond the saddle the area is also closed watershed land, so return by retracing your route.

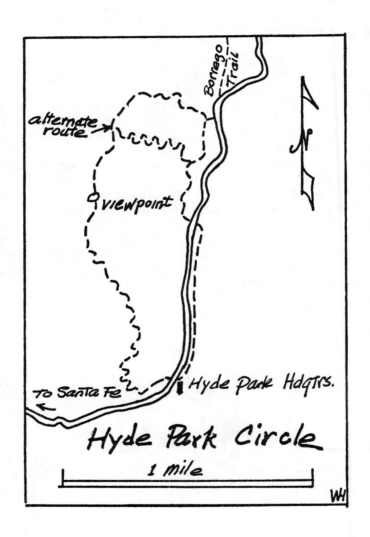

Hyde Park Circle
1 mile

WH

HYDE MEMORIAL PARK CIRCLE

by
John H. Muchmore

U.S. GEOLOGICAL SURVEY MAP REQUIRED: McClure Reservoir - 7.5 minute series (the trail described below is not shown on the map).

SALIENT FEATURES: Short, easy drive over paved road from Santa Fe. Well marked (blazes) and maintained trail. Includes Girl Scout nature trail. Site of early Santa Fe logging activity. Stands of piñon, ponderosa, spruce, fir, Gamble oak and wildflowers. Excellent 360 degree view includes Lake and Tesuque Peaks, the ski basin and the Sandia and Jemez Mountains. The real value of this walk will be obtained by strolling and stopping frequently.

RATING: Easy, but with steep trails.

ROUND TRIP HIKING DISTANCE: 5 miles.

APPROXIMATE HIKING TIME: 3 hours.

ALTITUDE RANGE: Highest point, 9400 feet; lowest point, 8400 feet; total vertical ascent, 1000 feet.

SEASONAL CONSIDERATIONS: Good four seasons walk, unless heavily snowed in.

ROUND TRIP DRIVING: 16 miles - approximately 45 minutes.

DRIVING DIRECTIONS: Leaving the main plaza, drive north on Washington Avenue 6 blocks and turn right on Artist Road. There is a sign here pointing to Hyde State Park and the Ski Basin. Measure your mileage from here. Artist Road becomes State Road 475 and you will see occasional green mileage markers as you continue uphill. Drive 7.2 miles to Hyde Memorial State Park Headquarters on your right. There are parking spaces in a large lot below the headquarters on the right-hand side of the road and in a smaller lot above the headquarters on the left side. Pay your entrance and use fees at the self-service payment box. The trail head is directly across from the stone store building and is marked with a direction sign.

HIKING INSTRUCTIONS: Begin your walk by crossing Little Tesuque Creek on the stone bridge opposite the general store, then turning left (south). The trail, well marked with tree blazes, climbs steeply through a series of switchbacks, then gradually levels off as it serpentines along an ascending ridge and finally tops out at a picnic area. It then begins a gradual descent traversing the east side of the ridge to a series of steep switchbacks that drop the trail to the north end of the park.

Check your watch as you cross the bridge, and plan to stop at half hour intervals to view the surrounding vistas and enjoy the distant mountains. At your first stop, you will be about 500 feet above the campground. Looking ahead to the northeast, you will see the Santa Fe Ski Basin with the watershed rising to Tesuque and Lake Peaks. Behind you to the southeast, Thompson Peak will be showing above the Black Canyon

notch.   At your next stop, northwest and
southwest views should have your attention.
Southwesterly   are   the   Sandia   and   Ortiz
Mountains.   Westerly and northwesterly are
the Jemez Peaks with the Buckman flats and
the Caja del Rio in the middle foreground.

Your trail now roller coasts along the ridge
and another five minutes brings you to a 360
degree view point.   There are two picnic
tables here that invite you to stop for
lunch or a snack.   Although downed timber
gives evidence of some harsh winter weather,
this trail's southern ascent makes it invit-
ing even during years of heavy snows. Turn-
of-the-century logging is evident along the
ridge.   A word of caution: During summer
thunderstorm   activity,   portions of this
ridge have taken direct lightning strikes.

As you continue along the ridge, you will
see a branch of the trail just beyond the
picnic tables.   This right-branching trail
will bring you down a series of switchbacks
to the recreational vehicle hookup section
of the Hyde Park Campground and will cut off
about 30 minutes of your walking circuit.
However, we suggest that you continue
straight ahead, omitting the right branch.
The main trail continues a gradual traversing descent along the northeast or right
side of the main ridge.

Within five minutes, your trail swings
sharply to the east (or your right) and
drops through a series of descending
switchbacks to the trail's end at the
northern boundary of the Hyde Park
Campground.   As you leave the trail, the
paved Ski Basin road will be directly in
front of you and can be followed down to
your car. Up the paved road, a hundred feet

or so to your left, is the present southern terminal of the Borrego Trail.

However, let us avoid the paved road. There are a series of short trails running down the canyon approximately 50 to 100 feet above the west side of the road. Keeping the paved road on your left, follow any of these interesting trails until you pass the recreational vehicle section. You will soon cross the alternate descending trail from the ridge above you. This trail almost immediately converges with the Girl Scout nature trail with its metal identification signs pointing out various types of trees, shrubs and wildflowers. The nature trail continues for about ten minutes and soon returns you to the paved road. At this point, cross the paved road, then Little Tesuque Creek, and then follow any of the dirt roads or trails that follow the creek back down to the Park Headquarters, the store and your car.

The entire circuit can be covered in three leisurely hours. With a picnic and a clear warm day the circuit could be extended to all day. Snow cover may require three strenuous hours for the circuit. Experienced hikers will walk this trail in under two hours. Novices should not attempt it in deep snow.

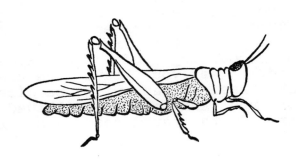

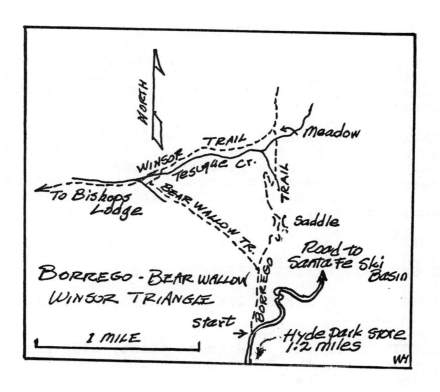

NORTH

WINSOR TRAIL

Meadow

Tesuque Cr.

BEAR WALLOW TR.

TRAIL

To Bishops Lodge

Saddle

BORREGO - BEAR WALLOW
WINSOR TRIANGLE

BORREGO

Road to Santa Fe Ski Basin

Start →

Hyde Park Store
1.2 miles

1 MILE

WH

BORREGO-BEAR WALLOW-WINSOR TRIANGLE

by
Bill Chudd

U.S. GEOLOGICAL SURVEY MAPS REQUIRED: Aspen Basin, and for the first five or six hundred yards only, McClure Reservoir - 7.5 minute series.

SALIENT FEATURES: An easily accessible short hike along good trails, partly stream-side, and through pleasant woods. You will make two stream crossings. If spring runoff is unusually high, the crossings can present some problems.

RATING: Easy.

ROUND TRIP HIKING DISTANCE: 4 miles.

APPROXIMATE HIKING TIME: 2 hours 15 minutes, with stops.

ALTITUDE RANGE: Highest point, 8880 feet; lowest point, 8240 feet; total vertical ascent, 760 feet.

SEASONAL CONSIDERATIONS: Usually snowed-in in midwinter. May be done at any other time. Can be hot in midsummer, but fairly well shaded.

ROUND TRIP DRIVING: 17.5 miles - approximately 40 minutes.

DRIVING DIRECTIONS: Leaving the main plaza, drive north on Washington Avenue 6 blocks and turn right on Artist Road. There is a sign here pointing to Hyde State Park and the Ski Basin. Measure your mileage from here. Artist Road becomes State Road 475 and you will see occasional green mileage markers as you continue uphill. Drive 8.3 miles to the Borrego trailhead. Look for a sign on the right side of the road reading "Borrego Trail Parking." Turn left into the paved parking lot.

HIKING INSTRUCTIONS: The trail starts down from the far left corner of the parking lot. There is a sign identifying this as the Borrego Trail, #150 and giving the distance to Big Tesuque Creek as one and a half miles. After 4 or 5 twists, the trail becomes wide and easy to follow. You have entered a lovely forest of firs, aspens and shortly, a few ponderosa pines. Later you may see some shrubby Gambel oaks trying valiantly to become full-fledged trees. The first part of the trail may show erosion due to new run-off patterns from the recently reconstructed Ski Basin road.

This is the Borrego Trail along which shepherds brought their flocks to market in Santa Fe from towns to the north, before modern roads and other developments made life easier and less interesting. In about a half mile the trail passes between two wooden signposts. If these remain intact, the left hand one will point out the Bear Wallow Trail, with Big Tesuque 1 mile away. The right hand sign will show the Borrego Trail, #150, with Big Tesuque ahead 1 1/4 miles, Aspen Ranch 5 miles and Hyde State Park 1/2 mile back. Take the left fork, the Bear Wallow Trail, #182, which heads west of

north.   After about 15 minutes you will get
glimpses   through the trees ahead of a trans-
verse ridge, indicating your approach to Big
Tesuque Creek.   Begin listening for the
always pleasant sound of its flow. Continue
down the switchbacks to the stream bank, one
mile from the Borrego Trail.

On the near bank is a sign pointing back
along Trail 182 to Hyde State Park. Cross
the creek to the west bank where you will
find the Winsor Trail, roughly paralleling
the creek.   There are two signs, generally
broken, one on a post, and another high on a
tree.   Your route will be upstream, a right
turn after crossing the creek.   If the
season is right, look around for raspberries
in this vicinity. Other berries you are apt
to encounter in the course of this hike are
strawberries (many plants but few berries);
edible (but not choice) thimbleberries; non-
poisonous (but hardly edible unless cooked
or prepared) Oregon grape and kinnikinnick;
and poisonous baneberry.

Make the right turn and continue on the
Winsor trail.   It's all upstream and uphill,
but you knew you'd have to pay for all that
lovely downhill trail behind you. Note the
ridge on your right, across the creek. Eventually, you're going to have to get over
that.   After one mile, a wooden post on each
side of the trail will identify the junction
of the Winsor and Borrego trails. The post
on the left has a sign giving distances to
Trail 182 (from which you have just come),
two other trails and to Bishops Lodge - 5
miles.   Another sign, higher up on a tree,
is identical, except that the distance to
Bishops Lodge is shown as 4.5 miles. Don't
try to figure it out.   The post on the
right, signless when I was last there,

should have a sign identifying the Borrego Trail. Turn right, southeast, onto the Borrego Trail. You will shortly cross the Big Tesuque Creek, and soon thereafter attack the ridge you saw earlier, by a winding switchback trail. After topping the ridge, the trail descends for a while, levels off, and then returns to the junction with Bear Wallow Trail which comes in from the right. You have now completed a triangle of the Bear Wallow, Winsor and Borrego Trails, each leg about one mile.

Continue on the Borrego Trail one-half mile to your car. Next time, take this circuit in the reverse direction. It will seem like a different walk.

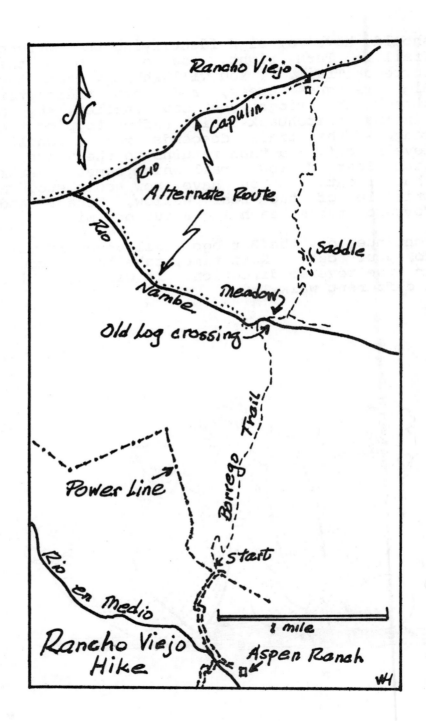

Rancho Viejo
Capulin
Rio
Alternate Route
Rio
Saddle
Nambe
Meadow
Old Log crossing
Borrego Trail
Power Line
Rio en Medio
start
1 mile
Rancho Viejo
Hike
Aspen Ranch
WH

-24-

RANCHO VIEJO

by
Betsy Fuller

U.S. GEOLOGICAL SURVEY MAP REQUIRED: Aspen Basin - 7.5 minute series.

SALIENT FEATURES: Lovely meadows and fast-running clear streams; wildflowers in season and good stands of ponderosa, spruce, fir, aspen. Not recommended for low-slung cars.

RATING: Moderate.

ROUND TRIP HIKING DISTANCE: 8.5 miles.

APPROXIMATE HIKING TIME: 5 hours.

ALTITUDE RANGE: Highest point, 9200 feet; lowest point, 8187 feet; total vertical ascent, 2300 feet.

SEASONAL CONSIDERATIONS: Not a winter hike.

ROUND TRIP DRIVING: 37 miles - approximately 2 hours.

DRIVING DIRECTIONS: Leaving the main plaza, drive north on Washington Avenue 6 blocks and turn right on Artist Road. There is a sign here pointing to Hyde State Park and the Ski Basin. Measure your mileage from here. Artist Road becomes State Road 475 and you will see occasional green mileage markers as you continue uphill. At 12 miles (1/2 mile beyond the Big Tesuque picnic area) turn left onto the Pacheco Canyon Road (Forest Road 102) and continue for 3 miles until the road comes to a "T" junction with Forest Road 412. Turn right on 412 and continue up and over a ridge into Aspen Ranch, which is a large open meadow area. The little bridge over the Rio en Medio is closed off here, so it will be necessary to turn left just before the bridge and ford the shallow creek. Keep on this road for another mile as it rises out of the Rio en Medio valley. When you come to a saddle where the road turns sharply to the right, you are at the trailhead. You will notice evidence of cars having parked here and a telephone line passes overhead. There may be a Forest Service sign here indicating Trail #150. If there isn't, look for the trail which starts downhill to the north.

Note: Front wheel drive cars with adequate clearance and four-wheel drive vehicles will have no problem on the road between the "T" and Aspen Ranch Meadow. Rear wheel drive and low-slung cars could encouter serious problems on this road, parts of which are heavily rutted. During the winter season the road from the Ski Basin down to the "T" (Forest Service #102) is closed to vehicular traffic and reserved for skiers only.

HIKING INSTRUCTIONS: Trail #150 starts downhill in a northerly direction. Take a deep breath of fresh mountain air (the altitude here is 9200 feet) and start down the trail. The Forest Service unimaginatively calls this Trail #150, but it is part of the old historic Borrego Trail which as recently as 50 years ago was used to herd sheep from the high mountains east of Chimayo and Truchas to Santa Fe. As you walk down the

small drainage, you'll be going through a
dark forest of spruce and fir. In the
summer, you may see the spectacular flowering green gentian, which sometimes grows as
tall as 5 feet, and if there is any water in
the small drainage, watch for the one-sided
pyrola in the wet dirt.

After about a mile and a half of steady descent, you'll first hear and then arrive at
the Rio Nambé which flows toward the west on
down to the Nambé Indian Pueblo about 6
miles downstream. Cross the river to the
north bank. For many years there has been a
huge fallen ponderosa pine lying across the
river from bank to bank. However, this log
has disintegrated to such an extent that by
the time this book is published, it will
surely be impassable for anyone bigger than
a chipmunk. Instead, you will have to cross
the river by wading across (and having wet
feet the rest of the trip) or by scouting up
and down the river for stepping stones or
another fallen log.

Just upstream from the crossing, you will
find yourself in a lovely open meadow. This
is a good spot for your first rest stop and
snack, especially since the next mile and a
half will involve climbing from an elevation
of about 8200 to 8800 feet. After your
rest, continue on upstream for about a quarter of a mile. At this point you will see
the trail divide, one branch going on up the
river and the other (still your Trail #150)
going to the left (north) up the slope away
from the river. You will be climbing
through ponderosa pines, and the trail is
lined with mountain mahogany which you can
identify by its curlicue seeds. As you top
the ridge and start down the trail on the
north facing slope into the Rio Capulin

(chokecherry) valley you'll be going through aspen forests and an occasional scrub oak grove.

It's approximately 2.5 miles from the Rio Nambé crossing where you had your snack, to the Rio Capulin. Walk downstream for a few hundred yards and you will find the burned out remains of an old log cabin that was once used by the sheepherders of the old Spanish ranch known as Rancho Viejo. Have a good rest in this lovely sloping meadow because retracing your steps back to your car will be more strenuous than the outbound trip, especially the long last ascent out of the Rio Nambé valley.

Someday, you may want to extend this walk by going downstream from the burned out cabin along the Rio Capulin to the junction of this stream with the Rio Nambé and then back up the Nambé to the fallen log near which you crossed several hours before. This added loop would increase your hike by about 3 miles.

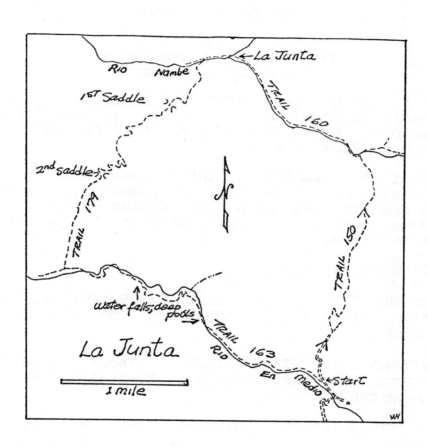

Rio Nambe

←La Junta

1st Saddle

TRAIL 160

2nd saddle

TRAIL 179

N

TRAIL 150

water falls, deep pools

TRAIL 163

La Junta

Rio

En medio

←Start

1 mile

WH

LA JUNTA CIRCUIT

by
Art Judd, E. J. Evangelos,
and John Jasper

U.S. GEOLOGICAL SURVEY MAP REQUIRED: Aspen Basin Quadrangle 7.5 minute series; other helpful maps: Santa Fe National Forest map, Pecos Wilderness map.

SALIENT FEATURES: Interesting hike in a little-used area with a number of stream crossings and with spectacular waterfalls, deep pools, and rock canyons. Strenuous elevations.

RATING: Strenuous.

ROUND TRIP HIKING DISTANCE: 9.2 miles, but the hike feels longer due to elevation changes.

APPROXIMATE HIKING TIME: About 6 hours, which does not include rest, meal and photo opportunity stops.

ALTITUDE RANGE: Highest point - 9200 feet; lowest point - 7640 feet; total vertical ascent - 2500 feet.

SEASONAL CONSIDERATIONS: Usually open May 1st to October 1st. This will vary depending upon snow conditions. River crossing could be difficult during the early spring run-off and the last part of the driving could be rutted, muddy and slippery during rainy or snowy weather.

ROUND TRIP DRIVING: Approximately 36 miles; 1 1/2 to 2 hours.

DRIVING DIRECTIONS: Leaving the main plaza, drive north on Washington Avenue 6 blocks and turn right on Artist Road. There is a sign here pointing to Hyde State Park and the Ski Basin. Measure your mileage from here. Artist Road becomes State Road 475 and you will see occasional green mileage markers as you continue uphill. At 12 miles (1/2 mile beyond the Big Tesuque picnic area) turn left onto the Pacheco Canyon Road (Forest Road 102) and continue for 3 miles until the road comes to a "T" junction with Forest Road 412. Turn right on 412 and continue up and over a ridge into Aspen Ranch, which is a large open meadow area. The little bridge over the Rio en Medio is closed off here, so it will be necessary to turn left just before the bridge and ford the shallow creek. Park at the signs at the end of the meadow.

Note: Front wheel drive cars with adequate clearance and four wheel drive vehicles will have no problem on Road 412 between the "T" and Aspen Ranch meadow. Rear wheel drive and low-slung cars could encounter serious problems on this road, parts of which are heavily rutted. During the winter season the road from the Ski Basin down to the "T" (Forest Road 102) is closed to vehicular traffic and reserved for skiers only.

HIKING INSTRUCTIONS: The hike starts up the dirt road you have just been driving on. Go uphill into the trees for about 3/4 mile to the trailhead which is usually marked by the

brown and white Forest Service sign indicating Trail 150. If the sign has been
destroyed, you will find the trailhead where
the road makes a sharp turn back to the
right at a saddle. A telephone line passes
overhead here and there is evidence of cars
having parked here.

From here you leave the road for the foot
trail which makes a steep descent for about
1.7 miles to the Rio Nambé. The Rio Nambé
begins to make itself heard as you near the
last quarter mile or so. Just before you
get to the river, notice the huge moss-
covered boulder on the left of the trail.
In the spring, garlands of wildflowers
bedeck this rock.

At the Rio Nambé, take Trail #160 downstream
for a few hundred yards and either ford the
river or cross on dead-fall. Continue on
down the river for about half an hour (a
little over a mile) to the junction of the
Rio Nambé with the Rio Capulin (La Junta
means the meeting point). You'll come to a
fork in the trail when you get close to this
junction. Take either one, they both lead
to La Junta. The Rio Capulin comes in from
the right. Cross it and continue on downstream for several hundred yards to the
junction of your trail (#160) with Trail
#179. A sign marking this junction is
tacked onto a large ponderosa pine, so watch
for it. Trail 179 crosses the river here.
Usually adequate dead-fall bridges the river
at this point. Cross with care, especially
in early spring and on frosty mornings, as
the tree trunks are often coated with ice
and can be very slippery.

After crossing the river, Trail 179 climbs
up a deeply scoured arroyo. In about 45

minutes on this trail, you'll top out at a saddle - a good place for a rest and a snack. The trail now turns downhill, passes through another valley and then ascends to the top of another saddle. At one place on this portion of the hike, the trail divides - take the left trail which switches back and forth to the second saddle. The power line crosses the trail here and you will now begin the one-mile descent to the Rio en Medio, a total of three miles from La Junta. Just before reaching the Rio en Medio, a trail sign states "Aspen Meadow 3 miles." A sharp left turn here onto Trail 163 will take you up the Rio en Medio to Aspen Ranch. At the junction, Trail 163 may be narrow and heavy with vegetation.

This is probably the most beautiful and strenuous leg of this lovely hike: three miles of waterfalls, deep pools, rock canyons, wildflowers, mushrooms, and trout. The trail back to Aspen Ranch crosses the Rio en Medio numerous times and goes steeply up to gain the elevation lost in the descent to La Junta. At one point where the trail crosses the river to the right, there is a large rock outcropping high above the river on the left which appears to be a sculpture of a woman with a shawl pulled partially over her head peering down into the river and perhaps weeping. Could this be La Llorona? After very steep climbing and much huffing and puffing, the trail levels out and ends back at Aspen Ranch Meadow and the cars.

To return to Santa Fe, either go back up the Pacheco Canyon Road the way you came or continue down Forest Road 412 past Vigil Meadows on the left to Rancho Encantado and the village of Tesuque and back to Santa Fe.

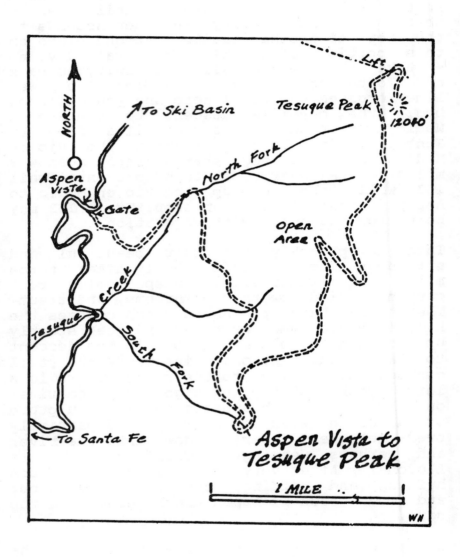

NORTH

↑To Ski Basin

Tesque Peak

Lift

12040'

Aspen Vista

←Gate

North Fork

Open Area

Creek

Tesuque

South Fork

← To Santa Fe

Aspen Vista to Tesuque Peak

1 MILE

WH

ASPEN VISTA TO TESUQUE PEAK

by
Walt Kunz

U.S.GEOLOGICAL SURVEY MAP REQUIRED: Aspen Basin - 7.5 minute series. The new topo map, revised in 1977, shows the road on which you will be walking. Older maps do not. A 'Visitor's Guide to the Pecos Wilderness' also shows the road, and is available from the Forest Service.

SALIENT FEATURES: Good stands of aspen, spruce and fir, clear streams, large open areas with excellent views. Trail is a somewhat maintained road. Especially beautiful in the fall when the aspens are golden. This is a popular and often crowded area at the height of the aspen viewing in late September and early October.

RATING: Strenuous.

ROUND TRIP HIKING DISTANCE: 12 miles.

APPROXIMATE HIKING TIME: 6 hours.

ALTITUDE RANGE: Highest point, 12,040 feet; lowest point, 10,000 feet; total vertical ascent, 2,040 feet.

SEASONAL CONSIDERATIONS: Usually snowed in at higher altitudes in winter and spring, but popular with cross country skiers in the winter. Even in July you may encounter snow. Bring adequate clothing.

ROUND TRIP DRIVING: 27 miles - approximately one hour.

DRIVING DIRECTIONS: Leaving the main plaza, drive north on Washington Avenue 6 blocks and turn right on Artist Road. There is a sign here pointing to Hyde State Park and the Ski Basin. Measure your mileage from here. Artist Road becomes State Road 475 and you will see occasional green mileage markers as you continue uphill. Drive 12.6 miles, then turn right onto a large parking lot marked by an identification sign.

HIKING INSTRUCTIONS: There is a gated access road on the east side of the parking area which is the start of the trail to Tesuque Peak. The "not for public use" sign refers to vehicles only; hiking (as well as cross country skiing) is permitted. This is the service road for the microwave relay station at the peak.

The first 2.5 miles are through aspen forest (spectacular in the fall); the last 3.5 miles are through fir and spruce alternating with large treeless areas. About 0.5 miles in you can catch a glimpse of your destination, the bare peak with microwave towers straight ahead. At 0.8 miles you cross the north fork of Big Tesuque Creek, at 1.6 miles, two more forks of the creek, and at 2.3 miles, the last fork. Water-loving flowers abound along the banks of the creeks. Late in the summer the lower stretches of the road are lined with masses of yellow senecio and purple asters.

Just past the last creek crossing, the road makes a switchback to the north (left) and enters a fir and spruce forest. At 3.8 miles the road traverses a large open area which affords good views of the Rio Grande valley north of Santa Fe, and a bit farther along, a panoramic view of Santa Fe.

At 5 miles, after a few more switchbacks, the road turns northeast and enters the forest again. In 1979, this section had about 3 feet of snow across the road in mid-July. At 5.5 miles the road enters another large open area. Below, to the northwest, you can see the top of a chair lift at the Santa Fe Ski Basin. The long fence straight ahead is a snow fence along one of the ski trails served by the ski lifts under which you will pass farther up the road. Above, to the northeast, are the microwave towers on Tesuque Peak, about 0.5 miles away by road.

At the top, the terrain drops steeply eastward into the Santa Fe River valley, a closed area which is a main part of Santa Fe's water supply. To the north is Lake Peak, about a mile away.

Return by the same route.

An alternate return route, with another car having been shuttled to and left at the Santa Fe Ski Basin, is to take one of the ski trails (if you know the trails) down to the ski basin parking lot. This maneuver would increase considerably the steepness of the descent but would shorten the hike by approximately 4 miles.

Fastest round trip time by runners is about one and a quarter hours.

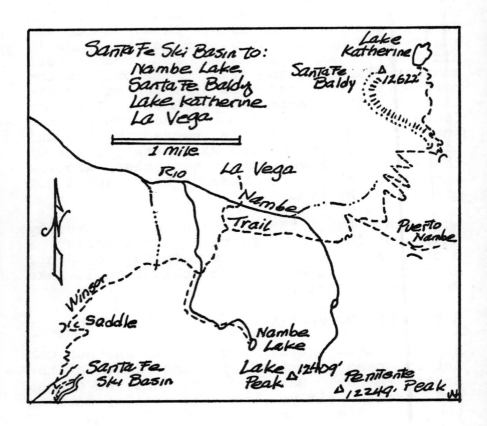

Santa Fe Ski Basin To:
Nambe Lake
Santa Fe Baldy
Lake Katherine
La Vega

1 mile

Lake Katherine

Santa Fe Baldy △ 12,622'

Rio

La Vega

Nambe Trail

Puerto Nambe

Winsor

Saddle

Nambe Lake

Santa Fe Ski Basin

Lake Peak △ 12,409'

Penitente Peak △ 12,249'

NAMBÉ LAKE

by
Carolyn Keskulla

U.S. GEOLOGICAL SURVEY MAP REQUIRED: Aspen Basin 7.5 minute series. See sketch map on page 38.

SALIENT FEATURES: You will have the special treat of seeing Nambé Lake which nestles under the cliff face of Lake Peak. Good hiking shoes are a necessity as the trail is very steep and in some places rocky as it climbs alongside Nambé Creek.

RATING: Moderate in distance, but there are some steep, rocky climbs.

ROUND TRIP HIKING DISTANCE: 7 miles.

APPROXIMATE HIKING TIME: About 5 hours, allowing time for lunch and a stroll around the lake.

ALTITUDE RANGE: Highest point, 11,400 feet; lowest point, 10,260 feet; total vertical ascent, 2,100 feet.

SEASONAL CONSIDERATIONS: Generally accessible from mid-June to mid-September. May be snowed-in at other times.

ROUND TRIP DRIVING: 30 miles; 1 hour, 20 minutes.

DRIVING DIRECTIONS: Leaving the main plaza, drive north on Washington Avenue 6 blocks and turn right on Artist Road. There is a sign here pointing to Hyde State Park and the Ski Basin. Measure your mileage from here. Artist Road becomes State Road 475 and you will see occasional green mileage markers as you continue uphill. Continue 14 miles to the Ski Basin and at the Ski Basin, keep to the left and park at the lower parking lot. Look for a sign that says "WINSOR TRAIL."

HIKING INSTRUCTIONS: After crossing the small wooden bridge, turn right and start uphill on the well-used Winsor Trail, #254. In a half mile or more of steep climbing you will be at the wilderness boundary fence, 560 feet higher than the trailhead. Watch for the lovely wildflowers among the aspen and spruce. In June you may see shooting star and fairy slipper orchid, among others. From the fence you start gently downhill passing, in about a quarter of a mile, a little noticed trail on the left. This is a very steep trail to the Rio Nambé nicknamed the "elevator shaft." Continue past it for about two miles from the start.

Just before dropping down an embankment to the river, you will find the trail going to the right (south) up alongside this lovely cascading alpine stream. There is no officially maintained trail to Nambé Lake which is hidden behind the high ridge to the southeast, but over the years, hikers have consistently used the easiest way up the stream to the lake. By using your own instinct and following the course of the stream and the fairly well-worn path, you will reach the lake, the source of the Rio Nambé.

The shallow lake nestles under the cliff
face of Lake Peak.   Flowers grow in profusion in July along the stream and around
the lake.   Parry's primrose, mertensia, and
marsh marigold are spectacular in early
July.   Later there will be fireweed, yampa,
monkshood and many others.

LA VEGA

by
Norbert Sperlich

U.S. GEOLOGICAL SURVEY MAP REQUIRED: Aspen Basin - 7.5 minute series. How to locate La Vega on the topo map? Find the Ski Area first. It is called "Santa Fe Recreation Area" on the map. Now find Aspen Peak (northwest of the Ski Area) and Santa Fe Baldy (northeast of the Ski Area). Place a ruler over the tops of Aspen Peak and Santa Fe Baldy. Starting at Santa Fe Baldy, follow the ruler down for 4 inches. You will come to a level area, indicated by the absence of contour lines. This is La Vega. The Spanish name translates into "meadow" or "pasture land." See sketch map on page 38.

SALIENT FEATURES: This hike through aspen, fir, and spruce takes you to an open meadow at the foot of Santa Fe Baldy. La Vega offers a beautiful setting away from the sometimes crowded Winsor Trail. Many wildflowers in season. Spectacular in late September and early October, when the aspens are golden.

RATING: Moderate.

ROUND TRIP HIKING DISTANCE: Approximately 7 miles.

APPROXIMATE HIKING TIME: 3 to 4 hours.

ALTITUDE RANGE: Highest point, 10,840 feet; lowest point, 10,000 feet; total vertical ascent, approximately 1,500 feet.

SEASONAL CONSIDERATIONS: Do not attempt this hike in snow or when visibility is poor.

ROUND TRIP DRIVING: 30 miles, about 1 hour and 20 minutes.

DRIVING DIRECTIONS: Leaving the main plaza, drive north on Washington Avenue 6 blocks and turn right on Artist Road. There is a sign here pointing to Hyde State Park and the Ski Basin. Measure your mileage from here. Artist Road becomes State Road 475 and you will see occasional green mileage markers as you continue uphill. Continue 14 miles to the Ski Basin and at the Ski Basin, keep to the left and park at the lower parking lot. Look for a sign that says "WINSOR TRAIL."

HIKING INSTRUCTIONS: From the trailhead, you will cross a small stream and go up on the Winsor Trail (to the right, Trail 254). The trail zigzags up through a forest of aspen, fir, and spruce trees and crosses several small meadows. After half an hour or so of steep climbing you come to a meadow and the entrance gate to the Pecos Wilderness. You have reached the highest point of the hike (10,840 feet). Time to catch your breath and to feed the Gray Jays that are usually waiting here for handouts from hikers.

The trail now descends gradually through stands of conifers and aspens. After about an hour of hiking time (from the Ski Basin) you will reach a clearing that is to the right of the trail. At this point, a smaller trail goes off to the right to Nambé Lake. (See page 39 for a description of the hike to Nambé Lake.) You will continue on the Winsor Trail which, right after the clearing, crosses Nambé Creek. Check the time at this point. In about ten minutes you will reach the turnoff to La Vega, a small trail that goes down to the left. Look for a sign high up on an aspen tree on the left side of the trail. The sign says, "LA VEGA SHORTCUT." Here, you leave the well-traveled Winsor Trail and take the trail to La Vega. This trail is not on the topo map!

For a while, the trail stays on top of a ridge, then it drops down into the valley to the right of the ridge. Keep your eyes on the trail. It is overgrown in some places and obstructed by fallen aspen trees in other places. At the valley bottom, the trail enters into a conifer forest and then comes to a stream (a tributary of the Nambé River). At this point, you have hiked for about 20 minutes on the La Vega Shortcut Trail. You have now reached the lowest point of the hike (approximately 10,000 feet). Cross the stream on a bridge of slippery logs. The trail now turns left and goes up on the other side of the creek. About 30 yards away from the stream, you will come to a sign on the right side of the trail. The sign is high up on an aspen tree and points in the direction from which you were coming. It says:

UPPER NAMBÉ TRAIL
WINSOR CR TRAIL 1/2 ->
SKI BASIN 3 ->

Immediately after the sign, your trail meets the Rio Nambé Trail. You take the left branch of the latter trail. For a while,

the trail descends slowly, with the stream
on your left within earshot. After a few
minutes, you will be going uphill again and
the trail moves to the right, away from the
stream. Some 15 minutes after passing the
last sign (near the creek), the trail will
take you up to a low ridge. Ahead of you is
a clearing and a sign post. The sign, about
chest high (likely to be destroyed by van-
dals) will tell you:

LA VEGA
<- RIO NAMBÉ TRAIL
<- BORREGO TRAIL 4
<- ASPEN RANCH 7

The trail is not clearly visible beyond this
point. Walk 10 yards or so past the sign
post, and you will look down on La Vega, a
large meadow (altitude about 10,100 feet)
interspersed with spruce and fir trees and
patches of gooseberry bushes. Opposite you,
to the north, the meadow is framed by two
ridges that lead up to Santa Fe Baldy. (The
top of Santa Fe Baldy is not visible from
this point.) A little stream comes down in
the valley between the two ridges and
meanders through the meadow, turning to the
west to join Nambé Creek further down. If
you are lucky, you might see deer bounding
across the meadow. More likely, you will
encounter a herd of grazing cattle.

Before you move on to explore La Vega or to
relax at the bank of the stream, memorize
the location of the LA VEGA sign post. You
will have to return to this post in order to
find the trail. When exploring the meadow,
watch out for swampy areas.

Start your return at the sign post and go
back the way you came. After a few minutes

of hiking you will hear the creek below you on the right. Once the creek comes into your view, watch for the turnoff to the right and the sign high up on an aspen tree. Turn to the right and go down to the stream. Cross the stream and retrace your steps back to the Winsor Trail. When you reach the Winsor Trail, turn right and go back to the Ski Basin.

SANTA FE BALDY

by
Arnold and Carolyn Keskulla

U.S. GEOLOGICAL SURVEY MAP REQUIRED: Aspen Basin - 7.5 minute series. See sketch map on page 38.

SALIENT FEATURES: You will experience the satisfaction of achieving the summit of a beautiful mountain with unsurpassed views, clear running streams and lovely wildflowers. There are steep grades and high altitudes. Pick a clear day to make your climb and be well equipped with full canteen, poncho, lunch and energy. This is a strenuous hike and you should be in good shape. Start as early as you can in order to be off the peak before the usual summer afternoon thunderstorms begin.

RATING: Strenuous.

ROUND TRIP HIKING DISTANCE: 12 or 13 miles.

APPROXIMATE HIKING TIME: 8 hours.

ALTITUDE RANGE: Highest point, 12,622 feet; lowest point, 10,260 feet; total vertical ascent, 2,760 feet.

SEASONAL CONSIDERATIONS: Generally accessible from mid-June to mid-September. Snowed-in at other times. The best time to climb Santa Fe Baldy is in late June or early July because the thunderstorm season may not have begun and the forget-me-nots and other alpine flowers are in profusion.

ROUND TRIP DRIVING: 30 miles - approximately 1 hour and 20 minutes.

DRIVING DIRECTIONS: Leaving the main plaza, drive north on Washington Avenue 6 blocks and turn right on Artist Road. There is a sign here pointing to Hyde State Park and the Ski Basin. Measure your mileage from here. Artist Road becomes State Road 475 and you will see occasional green mileage markers as you continue uphill. Drive 14 miles and when the paved road splits, keep straight ahead. Paved parking is located just ahead on your right in either of two parking lots. The trailhead is identified with a direction sign and a U.S. Forest Service bulletin board displaying a map of area trails and is directly ahead at the lower end of the largest parking lot.

HIKING INSTRUCTIONS: After crossing the small wooden bridge turn right and start uphill on the well-used Winsor Trail, #254. In a half mile or more of steep climbing you will be at the wilderness boundary fence, 560 feet higher than the trailhead. Watch for the lovely wild flowers among the aspen and spruce. In June you may see shooting star and fairy slipper orchid, among others. From the fence you start gently downhill passing in about a quarter of a mile a little noticed trail on the left. This is a very steep trail to the Rio Nambé nicknamed the "elevator shaft." Continue past it for about two miles from the start. Here a trail goes south up to lovely Nambé Lake beneath Lake Peak (see page 39 for the Nambé Lake hike). However, you go straight ahead across the Rio Nambé and continue along the Winsor Trail. After crossing two streams (which feed into the Rio Nambé), start up the switchbacks which will lead you to a trail junction at 11,000 feet, 4.5 miles from the Ski Basin. The level grassy meadow here is generally referred to as Puerto Nambé.

Take the left fork, Trail #251 (not shown on U.S.G.S. map) which leaves the Winsor Trail, and goes northeasterly up long switchbacks to the top of a saddle. From the saddle leave the trail and strike for the summit up the ridge to your left (north) by line of sight. There is no real trail.

This is a steep ascent, so you may have to make your own switchbacks and rest occasionally. There may be a few snow patches. Along with your lunch, enjoy the superb views from the top, and don't miss looking down on Lake Katherine by walking a short distance to the northeast. The unforgettable blue forget-me-nots, fairy primroses, sky pilots and other beautiful alpine flowers will be abundant early in the season. Later, bistorts, gentians, composites and others will appear. Remember to turn back at any sign of a thunderstorm. Before you leave the top check your bearings by sight or compass so that you can reach Puerto Nambé again, and the trail back to the ski basin. You have climbed to the summit of a 12,622 foot peak, an unforgettable experience!

LAKE KATHERINE

by
Kenneth D. Adam

U.S. GEOLOGICAL SURVEY MAPS REQUIRED: Aspen Basin and Cowles - 7.5 minute series. The current maps (Aspen Basin 1953 and Cowles 1961) do not show the trail from Puerto Nambé to Lake Katherine. See sketch map on page 38.

SALIENT FEATURES: A fine high altitude hike over well marked and graded trails through aspen, fir and spruce forest and high alpine meadows, ending in a beautiful alpine lake in a spectacular setting. Fine views of nearby peaks and distant valleys.

RATING: Strenuous.

ROUND TRIP HIKING DISTANCE: 14.5 miles.

APPROXIMATE HIKING TIME: 7 to 8 hours, plus time for stops.

ALTITUDE RANGE: Highest point, 11,750 feet; lowest point, 10,250 feet; total vertical ascent, 3,200 feet.

SEASONAL CONSIDERATIONS: Practical without skis from about early June, depending on snow, until the first major snowfall.

ROUND TRIP DRIVING: 30 miles - approximately 1 hour and 20 minutes.

DRIVING DIRECTIONS: Leaving the main plaza, drive north on Washington Avenue 6 blocks and turn right on Artist Road. There is a sign here pointing to Hyde State Park and the Ski Basin. Measure your mileage from here. Artist Road becomes State Road 475 and you will see occasional green mileage markers as you continue uphill. Continue 14 miles to the Ski Basin and at the Ski Basin, keep to the left and park at the lower parking lot. Look for a sign that says "WINSOR TRAIL."

HIKING INSTRUCTIONS: From the trailhead, immediately cross a small stream (the upper part of the Rio en Medio), turn right and start to climb. The trail starts with the steepest climb of the day through mixed aspen and conifer forest (very spectacular in the fall). After two or three switch-backs and a couple of small meadows (wild iris in season), you will arrive at the entrance gate of the Pecos Wilderness in a meadow at the top of the first climb. This pass is between the watersheds of the Rio en Medio and Rio Nambé. The elevation here is 10,850 feet. The trail now traverses the north slope of the divide, gradually losing altitude for about 1.5 miles until it reaches a sparkling stream, Nambé Creek. You will have been walking about one hour at this point. The trail continues to tra-verse, without much altitude change, to the northeast.

Keep to the main (Winsor) trail, T-254, now climbing slightly through aspen groves and small meadows. You will cross three minor streams and pass by two places where trails lead off to the left from the main trail. Stay on the main trail, Winsor Creek Trail, No. 254. The three quarters of a mile uphill stretch from the last stream to

Puerto Nambé will seem more like a mile.
After twenty or twenty five minutes you will
finally reach the "Y" trail junction at
Puerto Nambé in a beautiful high meadow.
Fine views of Santa Fe Baldy to the north
and Lake Peak and Penitente Peak to the
south and southeast may be seen. While you
stop to rest at the junction several Gray
Jays will probably pester you for a hand-
out. With just a little patience on your
part, they will eat from your hand.

You now leave the Winsor Creek Trail and
take Sky Line Trail, the left trail at the
"Y." From here on, the trail is not shown
on the U.S.G.S. topo map. It crosses the
meadow and starts up a series of long, long
switchbacks which finally bring you to the
divide between the Rio Nambé and Pecos watersheds. You will have been walking about
three hours at this point. This is a wonderful rest/snack spot with dramatic scenery in
all directions; the upper Pecos basin to the
east, the Rio Grande valley and Jemez Mountains to the west, Santa Fe Baldy right next
to you on the northwest and Lake Peak and
Penitente Peak to the south and southeast.

You are at the edge of a steep dropoff to
the east, and looking down you can see the
trail zigging and zagging down in a series
of seven switchbacks. After dropping down
these switchbacks, the trail starts a
climbing traverse to the northwest across
the upper edge of a large talus slope, then
through open forest. Level stretches of
trail are interrupted with short climbs up
switchbacks. Be on the look-out for abrupt
changes in trail direction that mark switchbacks. You finally leave the forest and
cross an open talus-covered area. The trail
is not very definite here. At the end of the

talus area is a sign reading "Lake Katherine," although you cannot yet see the lake. A short walk through open forest brings you to the eastern shoreline of Lake Katherine, elevation 11,742 feet. You are in a high alpine bowl, with Santa Fe Baldy directly above you to the southwest. It looks so close that you will be tempted to climb it on your way home. This can be done by climbing the steep grassy slope above the west shore of the lake and following the ridge to the summit. It involves an extra 900 feet of climbing at high altitude, however, and is definitely not recommended unless every member of your party is in excellent shape and you know your way back from the summit. The recommended return is by retracing your route in reverse.

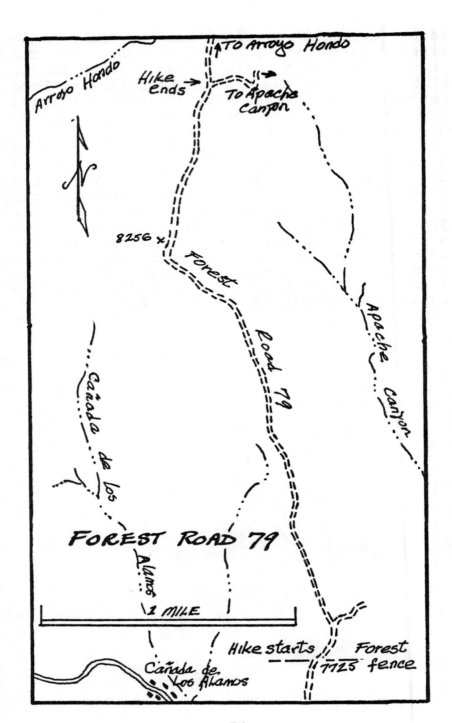

Arroyo Hondo

To Arroyo Hondo

Hike Ends

To Apache Canyon

8256 x

Forest

Road 79

Apache Canyon

Cañada de los

FOREST ROAD 79

Alamos

1 MILE

Hike starts

Forest

Cañada de Los Alamos

7725 fence

FOREST SERVICE ROAD #79

by
Wesley Horner

U.S. GEOLOGICAL SURVEY MAPS REQUIRED:
Glorieta and McClure Reservoir - 7.5 minute series.

SALIENT FEATURES: A pleasant road walk within the Santa Fe National Forest in the foothills near Santa Fe, with gentle grades, following a long ridge covered with open ponderosa pine woods providing excellent views in every direction.

RATING: Easy.

ROUND TRIP HIKING DISTANCE: 5 1/2 miles.

APPROXIMATE HIKING TIME: 2 1/2 - 3 hours.

ALTITUDE RANGE: Lowest point, 7,700 feet; highest point, 8,260 feet; total vertical ascent, 560 feet.

SEASONAL CONSIDERATIONS: Year round hike.

ROUND TRIP DRIVING: 24 miles, one hour.

DRIVING DIRECTIONS: From Santa Fe, drive south on Old Santa Fe Trail onto Old Pecos Trail to a stop light at the intersection of the Old Las Vegas Highway (signed). At the light take a left turn to the Old Las Vegas Highway. About 3 miles from this light look for a sign indicating the turn-off to Cañada de los Alamos and Camp Stoney. Turn left here. Once on this road, look for Forest Road 79 signs. At this point you are 5 miles from the start of the hike. Go about 0.9 miles to a T intersection. Turn right, following the main road to a Y where the Camp Stoney road goes straight ahead. Take the left hand fork down the hill to and through the village of Cañada de los Alamos, continuing along the road, which at times serves as a stream bed. Follow the road as it turns left sharply uphill. Cross the cattle guard and continue left when the road splits. Pass the Santa Fe Treehouse Camp (SFTHC) on your right, a short distance beyond which is the Forest Boundary cattle guard, where the hike begins.

There is ample parking space on the left before crossing the cattle guard, or on the right after crossing it.

HIKING INSTRUCTIONS: Immediately past the cattle guard, bear left. (The right-hand fork goes to the private Apache Creek development.) As the road follows an open ridge it affords fine views in all directions. To the east, on your right side, is the aptly named Shaggy Peak, covered with bold outcrops of pre-Cambrian granite and gneiss, the same rock forming the ridge and underlying the surrounding area. On the skyline behind is a high ridge whose two prominent summits are Glorieta Baldy and, farther to the north, Thompson Peak. In the far distance to the northeast are the higher peaks of the Sangre de Cristo Range, snow-patched during most of the year. To the southwest lie the low foothills of the Cerros Negros, and beyond are the Ortiz Mountains and the Cerrillos Hills, where gold and turquoise, respectively, have been mined for centuries. On the far horizon are the Sandias, standing just east of Albuquerque, and more toward the west, Mt. Taylor, an isolated volcanic pile, over a hundred miles away near Grants, New Mexico.

The walk is made especially pleasant by the easy footing and by the ponderosa pine forest through which the road passes. Selective timber cutting about ten years ago has opened the woods for the continued healthy growth of those trees left, as well as for the numerous new ones. There is little underbrush, so the needle carpet forms a smooth gray cover on the forest floor. Since the ridge is high and open, the wind is usually whispering through the pines.

The highest point in the hike is reached about 2 miles from the start where the elevations is 8,256 feet, marked by the USGS benchmark HONDO, a low square concrete pillar topped with a brass marker, standing about 20 feet off to the left. Here the road turns to the right and continues to follow the ridge for about another half mile to the end of the hike, marked by a sign which says "Dead End Road." The mountain straight ahead is Sierra Pelada. The dead end road (Forest Service), which can be followed as a continuation of this hike, leads over into Apache Canyon about two miles north. The narrow road straight ahead goes down into the head of Arroyo Hondo.

At the high point on your return to your car you will see in the distance to the southeast vast waves of gently southward sloping high mesas, formed by Mesozoic sandstone and shale strata, marking the southern end of the Sangre de Cristo uplift.

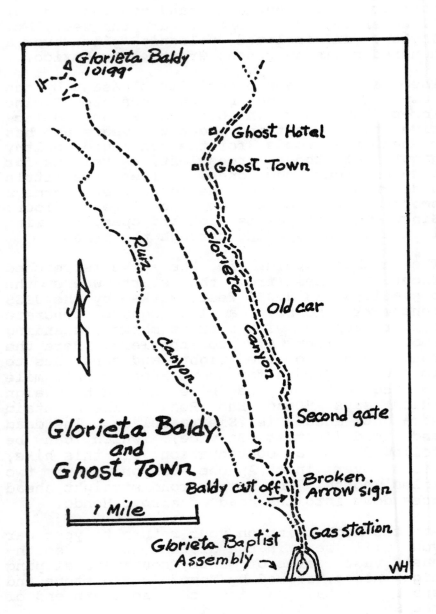

Glorieta Baldy
10199'

Ghost Hotel

Ghost Town

Ruiz

Glorieta

Canyon

Canyon

old car

Second gate

Glorieta Baldy
and
Ghost Town

Baldy cut off

Broken
Arrow sign

1 Mile

Glorieta Baptist
Assembly

Gas station

WH

GLORIETA BALDY

by
Bill Chudd

U.S. GEOLOGICAL SURVEY MAPS REQUIRED: Glorieta and McClure Reservoir - 7.5 minute series. Caution - there is a trail shown on these maps which is NOT the current trail and which took an entirely different route to the summit. The present trail is not shown. It approaches the summit along a ridge between Glorieta Canyon to the east, and Ruiz Canyon to the west. At this writing, a map prepared by the U.S.G.S. and the Safety-Security Unit of the Glorieta Conference Center is available at the trailhead. The upper trail is not shown in detail as to the final switchbacks and approach to the lookout tower. If you lose the trail, the U.S.G.S. topo maps, a compass, an altimeter, and your skills will permit you to retain your orientation and to find your way.

SALIENT FEATURES: Easy approach on paved roads to the wilderness trailhead. A steady uphill trail, quite steep in places, to a 10,200 foot peak with a fire lookout tower. Intimations of heaven and sweeping views of earth. Downhill all the way back. Carry sufficient water.

RATING: Strenuous.

ROUND TRIP HIKING DISTANCE: Rated at 10.2 miles on the map provided at the trailhead

and at 14 miles on the roadside sign on
Apple Street. My estimate: 11 steep, strenuous, and satisfying miles.

APPROXIMATE HIKING TIME: 6 hours - roughly
3.5 hours up and 2.25 hours down. Because
of the steady, steep ascent, this will vary
according to the condition of the hikers.

ALTITUDE RANGE: Highest point, 10,199 feet;
lowest point, 7,475 feet; total vertical
ascent, 2,800 feet.

SEASONAL CONSIDERATIONS: An excellent
spring, summer and fall walk. The early
part of the trail may be hard to follow when
snow covered. Likely to be heavily snowed
in in midwinter. In summer start early
enough to be off the peak shortly after noon
to avoid the afternoon lightning storms.

ROUND TRIP DRIVING: 40 miles - about an
hour.

DRIVING DIRECTIONS: Take I-25 north, toward
Las Vegas, to exit #299 at Glorieta. Following the direction signs for the Glorieta
Baptist Conference Center, turn left at the
top of the ramp. At the barrier, turn left
again, paralleling the highway, to the gatehouse of the Conference Center. Stop at the
gatehouse and if there is a security officer
there advise him or her of your hike plan.

On leaving the gatehouse, immediately turn
right onto Oak Street. Follow Oak Street
through the conference grounds. At .6 miles
from the gate, Oak Street turns right. Do
not go straight ahead, a move which would
mislead you onto Willow Street, but continue
on Oak Street to the right. There is a
small street sign at this street fork. At

.9 miles, after passing the firehouse on your right, turn right onto Apple Street. There are three signs at this intersection, a Conoco sign, a Glorieta Mini-Mart sign, and a Baldy Trail sign.

The first building on the left on Apple Street is a gas station. Turn left here to a grassy area beyond the last gas pump, and park off the pavement on the grass.

(Note: Driving back from the parking area, you may want to turn right from Apple Street onto Oak Street, which completes a circle of the Conference Center grounds and returns you to the entrance gate.)

HIKING INSTRUCTIONS: Start along the dirt roadway, a continuation of Apple Street, heading north. In about 200 yards you will come to a fence with a trail register at the left of the road. Register your hike, pick up a trail map, if available, and continue along the road. In another 200 yards you will see a prominent sign pointing out the trail to Broken Arrow and Glorieta Baldy on your left and to Ghost Town straight ahead. Leave the road, turning onto the trail to your left.

The lower part of the trail has been newly established as the route to the summit. It is reasonably well worn, but may be diffi- cult to follow when there is snow on the ground. Less than a quarter of a mile after the Broken Arrow sign, the uphill trail levels off among large boulders and seems to end. White arrows painted on the rocks and later on trees will direct you to your right, over the boulders, to the contin- uation of the trail. Study this area carefully. It is easy to get lost here on the return trip.

Further along the trail there may be some faded orange ribbons tied to bushes and tree branches. These were installed as temporary trail markers until the trail becomes sufficiently well worn.

After a number of small switchbacks, about a mile from the start, you will reach a sign pointing out the trail to Broken Arrow taking off to the right and your trail to Glorieta Baldy straight ahead. The trail keeps climbing mildly, with nice views toward the west (on your left). In the distance, behind a ridge, you will be able to identify the top of Shaggy Peak. Shortly, you will reach the top of a ridge, a good place to get your bearings. Eastward, to your right, you will be looking down into Glorieta Canyon. Westward, to your left, is a side canyon out of Ruiz Canyon. You are just above the mouth of this canyon which continues northward for a while between you and Ruiz. The trail follows the top of the ridge, climbing very gently.

About a mile and a half into the walk you will pass the point where the former lower part of this trail merges in from the right. There is a sign pointing back toward the trailhead and ahead to Glorieta Baldy. There is also a "Trail Closed" sign on the former trail. After this junction the trail widens and becomes progressively steeper. The ridge, too, widens until you are simply climbing up a hillside. You may still be able to spot old cut blazes and white or orange painted blaze markers on some tree trunks. The angle of climb continues to increase except at one point where the trail, narrow here, descends for a short distance to cross a drainage ravine, then

starts climbing again along the opposite
side.

The ponderosa pines have given way to firs
and at about 9,500 feet, patches of aspen
appear. These will announce themselves with
shouting golden hues in late September and
October. From time to time you will get
dramatic views back toward Glorieta and an
occasional view of the lookout tower ahead
through the tree tops.

The slope becomes quite steep as you approach the summit, with the trail switching
back and forth, crossing and recrossing a
steeper natural drainage channel with which
it can sometimes be confused. Should you
get onto this channel and find yourself
climbing directly skyward, you may continue
until you intersect the next trail switchback. There are small orange flags (the
type used for buried cable or pipe) here and
there along the switchbacks. If these are
maintained they will help you stay on the
trail.

A few hundred feet from the lookout tower a
trail comes in from the left. Turn right
and proceed to the base of the tower.
Before making the turn note this junction
well and when starting down be sure you do
not miss the left turn back onto the trail
you came up.

Look around. Wasn't it worth it? I've sat
here on a day with broken clouds rolling
below, revealing glimpses of hilltops, mesas
and distant plains, as though looking down
from heaven. On another unheavenly, still
day with a temperature inversion, I looked
to the southwest to see Albuquerque smog
snaking around the north slopes of Sandia

Mountain and sending a gray brown plume out over the plains to the east. It's an ever-changing, always remarkable view.

After descending, on the same trail, you may want to do a bit of sightseeing around the Glorieta Baptist Conference Center, an interesting city in the wilderness.

GLORIETA GHOST TOWN

by
Bill Chudd

U.S. GEOLOGICAL SURVEY MAPS REQUIRED: Glorieta and McClure Reservoir - 7.5 minute series. This hike appears on these maps as the lower part of an old trail to Glorieta Peak. That trail has long been abandoned and no longer exists. See sketch map on page 58.

SALIENT FEATURES: An easy-to-reach trail along a forest stream in Glorieta Canyon to a "ghost town." I have been told there was a lumber mill at the ghost town 40 or 50 years ago. You will see a large pile of lumber mill tailings. The only remaining ruins are that of a two-story log hotel and one other wooden building. A secluded walk through mixed conifer and deciduous woods. Some aspens and oaks pick up the sunlight in the autumn and provide touches of gold and reddish brown. Small meadows along the way contain a good mix of wildflowers in season. The geologic strata start with sandstone, followed by fossil-bearing limestone, and finally granite-like cliffs. The trail may be heavily used on some days, empty on others.

RATING: Moderate, bordering on easy.

ROUND TRIP HIKING DISTANCE: Just short of 6.5 miles.

APPROXIMATE HIKING TIME: 3 1/2 hours.

ALTITUDE RANGE: Highest point - 8420 feet; lowest point - 7475 feet; total vertical ascent, 950 feet.

SEASONAL CONSIDERATIONS: This can be an all-year walk, although accessibility in winter will depend on the amount of snowfall. The stream flow varies widely with the seasons. It may present difficult crossings at the height of the spring run-off or may be completely dry after prolonged drought.

ROUND TRIP DRIVING: 40 miles, one hour.

DRIVING DIRECTIONS: Take I-25 north, toward Las Vegas, to exit #299 at Glorieta. Following the direction signs for the Glorieta Baptist Conference Center, turn left at the top of the ramp. At the barrier, turn left again, paralleling the highway, to the gatehouse of the Conference Center. Stop at the gatehouse and if there is a security officer there advise him or her of your hike plan.

On leaving the gatehouse, immediately turn right onto Oak Street. Follow Oak Street through the conference grounds. At .6 miles from the gate, Oak Street turns right. Do not go straight ahead, a move which would mislead you onto Willow Street. There is a small street sign at this street fork. At .9 miles, after passing the firehouse on your right, turn right onto Apple Street. There are three signs at this intersection, a Conoco sign, a Glorieta Mini-Mart sign, and a Baldy Trail sign.

The first building on the left on Apple Street is a gas station. Turn left here to a grassy area beyond the last gas pump, and park off the pavement on the grass.

(Note: Driving back from the parking area,
you may want to turn right from Apple Street
onto Oak Street, which completes a circle of
the Conference Center grounds and returns
you to the entrance gate.)

HIKING   INSTRUCTIONS: Start along the dirt
roadway,   a   continuation   of   Apple   Street,
heading   north.   In about two hundred yards
you   will   reach   a   fence,   with   a   trail
register   at   the   left   of   the road.   After
registering   your   hike,   continue   along the
road.   Soon   a   sign marking the turnoff to
Broken   Arrow   and   to Glorieta Baldy and the
road   straight   ahead   to Ghost Town will re-
assure   you   that   you are on the right road.
About   a   quarter   of a mile past this sign a
new   road   has   been   constructed   to   a site
where   a   well   is being drilled.   It is easy
to   mistake   the new road for the road to the
ghost   town.   The road you want appears to be
a   small,   primitive   branch   road   coming in
from   the   left.   There   is   a   low, easily
missed   sign here with an arrow marked "Ghost
Town."   Watch for it carefully.   Should you
miss   it   and   find   yourself   at a dead end,
scout   out   the   area to your left.   Your road
is about 100 feet away.

Many   of   the common local wildflowers can be
seen   beside   the   road   on the early part of
the   walk.   About   a half mile in, you will
come   to   a   fence with an open field beyond.
The   field   has a heavy growth of mullein and
also   contains   some   yellow   or   yellow and
brown   prairie coneflowers, not too common in
our area.

Beyond   the field, just before the road turns
toward   the   right,   you   will again be reas-
sured   by   a   sign   pointing   back toward the
trailhead   and   ahead   to Ghost Town.   An old
trail   taking   off   to the left is marked by a

"trail closed" sign. This is a former trail to Glorieta Baldy, but not the original one shown on the USGS topo map. You will now be walking along what remains of the road to the old "Ghost Hotel." It climbs gradually. While the ascent totals about 900 feet, there are no really steep parts. The good news is that it's downhill all the way back.

You will begin to notice a small stream roughly paralleling the trail. It will stay with you all the way but here and there will take off for a little while, probably to get you to appreciate it more when it returns. You will cross the stream from time to time and, in places where it has eroded the road, take streamside paths or even walk 20 or 30 feet in the stream itself. The water is usually quite shallow.

At about three miles the first of the two ruins, that of an old wooden building, will appear at your left. Here the trail narrows to a thin path through the meadow between the ruin and the stream, then broadens again to the width of a primitive road. In less than a half mile you will reach another meadow. The ridge to your right across the stream features towering cliffs. Ahead and to your left, at the northwest end of the field is your destination, "Ghost Hotel."

Sit a while. Enjoy a snack. Looking at the cliffs to the east, across the stream, imagine, as I did, a colorful sunrise over these hills at the time the Ghost Hotel was in its heyday.

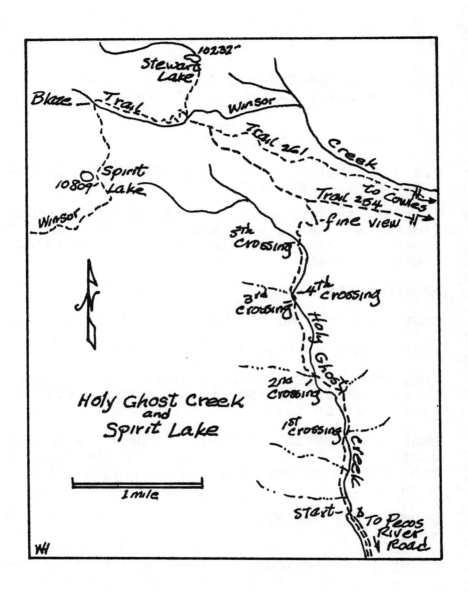

Holy Ghost Creek
and
Spirit Lake

1 mile

HOLY GHOST CREEK AND SPIRIT LAKE
(The Espiritu Santo Walk)

by
Carl Overhage

U.S. GEOLOGICAL SURVEY MAP REQUIRED: Cowles - 7.5 minute series.

SALIENT FEATURES: A walk uphill through flowering meadows, aspen groves, spruce forest, past a cascading stream, to a lovely mountain lake.

RATING: Strenuous.

ROUND TRIP HIKING DISTANCE: 14 miles.

APPROXIMATE HIKING TIME: 9 hours.

ALTITUDE RANGE: Highest point, 10,800 feet; lowest point, 8,150 feet; total vertical ascent, 2,750 feet.

SEASONAL CONSIDERATIONS: Summer and fall until the first snow. Early in the season, the stream crossings may be difficult due to snow melt.

ROUND TRIP DRIVING: 81 miles - approximately 3 hours.

DRIVING DIRECTIONS: From Santa Fe drive north on I-25 toward Las Vegas, New Mexico, for approximately 15 miles and exit on the Glorieta off-ramp #299. Turn left on the overpass, then turn right on State Road 50 and drive 6 miles to the town of Pecos. At the stop sign turn left onto State Road 63 which leads north into the Pecos River valley. Measure your mileage from this stop sign. Drive 13.5 miles to the Terrero bridge. Just before reaching the bridge, swing left on Forest Road 122 leading to Holy Ghost Campground. There is a direction sign at this intersection. Drive about 3 miles to the end of this road and park.

HIKING INSTRUCTIONS: The trail begins on the right side of the parking area for hikers. The trail crosses the stream on a foot bridge, and then follows Holy Ghost Creek upstream. After passing through some large meadows for about twenty minutes, you will cross Holy Ghost Creek from west to east. Another twenty minutes takes you to the second crossing and back to the west bank. In the meantime, you will have seen many wildflowers, and you will have been greatly tempted to linger among them.

Next, you have a short steep climb up a ridge. You come to some aspen groves with beautiful fern; then you descend to the creek. After crossing it twice, you will be back on the west bank. You pass a grassy clearing surrounded by aspens, and soon afterwards cross the creek for the fifth time.

Once on the east bank, you turn away from the stream and begin the climb up the ridge between Holy Ghost Creek and Winsor Creek. During the next half hour, by a series of switchbacks, you will gain 650 feet in elevation. On the way up, you pass a small promontory, from which there is a fine view down into the Holy Ghost valley. You reach

the top of a ridge and, at the northwest end
of a fine meadow, the intersection with a
trail (Tr. 254) coming up from Cowles. You
are now three hours away from the starting
point, and this is a good place to rest for
a brief snack.

The walk continues in a northwesterly direction through beautiful forest land. In
about thirty minutes you come to the intersection with another (shorter) trail (Tr.
261) from Cowles coming up on your right.
Fifteen minutes later, you come to a point
where you cross the main branch of Winsor
Creek, which descends from Lake Katherine.
After crossing the creek to its north bank,
the trail splits in two. The Winsor Trail
to Spirit Lake bears left, toward west.
(The trail to the right goes north to
Stewart Lake, less than half an hour away,
and only one hundred feet above this
junction. If you feel tired at this time,
you may decide to go to Stewart Lake,
instead of walking more than one hour and
climbing seven hundred feet to Spirit Lake.)

After leaving the Winsor Creek crossing, the
trail to Spirit Lake climbs fairly steeply,
following Winsor Creek upstream. In several
places, you get beautiful views of the
stream as it cascades down its steep
course. The trail becomes gradually easier
as it passes some lush green meadows a short
distance to the left. Twenty minutes after
leaving the Winsor Creek crossing, you
should begin to look for a trail junction,
where the trail to Lake Katherine takes off
to the right. In 1989, this junction still
had a signpost.

The Winsor Trail to Spirit Lake continues
straight ahead. In five minutes, you will

come to a somewhat confusing spot, where the trail crosses Winsor Creek from its north bank to the south bank. As you come closer to the creek, keep looking at the opposite bank for a blaze on a large spruce and for a low cairn. This marks the place where the Winsor Trail crosses to the south bank. Disregard the abandoned former Lake Katherine trail, which continues up the north side of Winsor Creek. Once across the creek, the trail is easy to follow as it climbs up the low ridge separating the Winsor and Holy Ghost drainages. You will reach the lake about half an hour after the last Winsor Creek crossing, and about five hours from the beginning of the walk.

The return trip will present no special problems. At the junctions with the trails from Cowles, remember to keep right. Shortly after the third crossing of Holy Ghost Creek on the return walk, as you walk parallel to the stream on its right (west) bank, you will come to a trail fork which you may not have noticed in the morning on the way up. Take the right branch, which goes up steeply for a short distance. On the home stretch through the streamside meadows, you may now feel that you have time for a more leisurely look at the many wildflowers.

Note: John Muchmore's helpful observations during joint walks over this route are gratefully acknowledged.

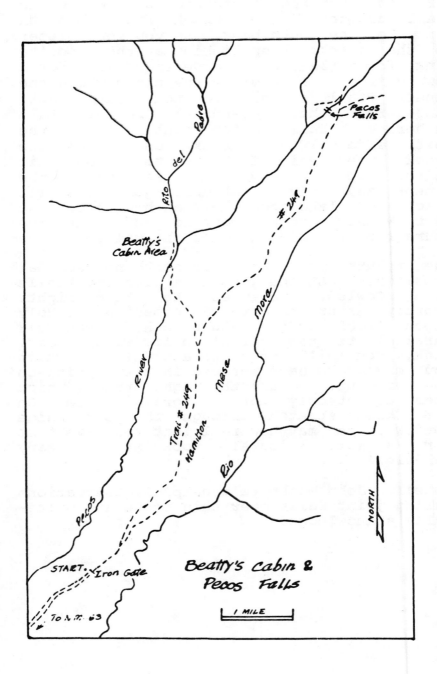

Beatty's Cabin &
Pecos Falls

1 MILE

-74-

BEATTY'S CABIN
and
PECOS FALLS
(as an optional extension)

by
Philip L. Shultz

U.S. GEOLOGICAL SURVEY MAPS REQUIRED: Pecos Falls and Elk mountain - 7.5 minute series.

SALIENT FEATURES: This hike goes through some of the most beautiful high meadows of the Pecos Wilderness, with outstanding views of the Truchas Peaks, Pecos Baldy and Lake Peak from the east side. In early summer the irises are spectacular.

RATING: Beatty's Cabin, strenuous; Pecos Falls, very strenuous.

ROUND TRIP HIKING DISTANCE: Beatty's Cabin, 10 miles; Pecos Falls, 17 miles.

APPROXIMATE HIKING TIME: Beatty's Cabin, 4.5 hours; Pecos Falls, 8 hours.

ALTITUDE RANGE: For Beatty's Cabin: Highest point, 10,200 feet; lowest point, 9,400 feet; total vertical ascent, 1,640 feet. For Pecos Falls: Highest point, 10,600 feet; lowest point, 9,400 feet; total vertical ascent, 1,300 feet.

SEASONAL CONSIDERATIONS: This is not a winter hike. Four-wheel drive is required whenever the road is likely to be muddy.

ROUND TRIP DRIVING: 94 miles - approximately 3.5 hours.

DRIVING DIRECTIONS: From Santa Fe drive north on I-25 toward Las Vegas, New Mexico, for approximately 15 miles and exit on the Glorieta off-ramp #299. Turn left on the overpass, then turn right on State Road 50 and drive 6 miles to the town of Pecos. At the stop sign turn left onto State Road 63 which leads north into the Pecos River valley. Measure your mileage from this stop sign. From the Pecos stop sign, drive 18.5 miles, passing several camp and picnic grounds and the little settlement of Terrero where the pavement ends and a dirt road continues. At the top of a grade turn right on Forest Road 223. A sign here will direct you to Iron Gate Campground. The distance between this junction and the campground is 4 miles; the road is steep and rough in places. Four-wheel drive is essential when the road is wet and muddy. (Remember the road may be dry in the morning but wet in the afternoon when you return after a summer shower.) Near the far end of the campground you will find a parking area on the right for hikers.

HIKING INSTRUCTIONS: The trail starts at the far end of the campground. Trail 249 gently zigzags northeast from the gate at the Iron Gate Campground. It rises about 300 feet in a little under half a mile, through spruce, fir and aspen to a usually well marked junction with Trail 250 which goes essentially straight and makes up the right fork of the junction. Remain on Trail 249, bearing slightly left and still climbing. This is a popular trail for hikers and horsemen, so the trail marker signs may be torn down or defaced. In another quarter of a mile or so the trail comes out of the aspen, still climbing gently through the first meadow. In June the irises are gorgeous for the next 2 miles. Also, look for mariposa lilies. Kestrels are rather common and I have seen elk in these meadows on several occasions. The trail tops out at about 10,200 feet. This is a beautiful point for the first hour's rest, with fine views of the Truchas Peaks to the north. Three and a half miles from the start is the next marked trail junction, and the point of decision of whether to do the very long walk to Pecos Falls.

If you decide on the shorter trip to Beatty's Cabin, bear left (downhill to the northwest), entering the woods promptly for the winding descent to the Pecos River. Cross the good bridge and find a spot on the lovely grassy slope for a rest. The actual cabin is long gone. It was upstream near the confluence with the Rito del Padre. Return by the same route for a lovely, not too strenuous hike.

If you decide on the longer trip to Pecos Falls, instead of taking the left-hand trail to Beatty's Cabin, bear right on your original Trail 249. The trail generally follows the 10,200 foot contour through meadows and islands of aspen for about 4 miles to the falls, which are quite beautiful during the spring runoff when there is a good stream flowing. Return by retracing your walk along Trail 249 all the way back to Iron Gate Campground.

This wonderful high country is at its best in early summer when the irises are at their height, and in late September when the aspen leaves are golden. Enjoy it!

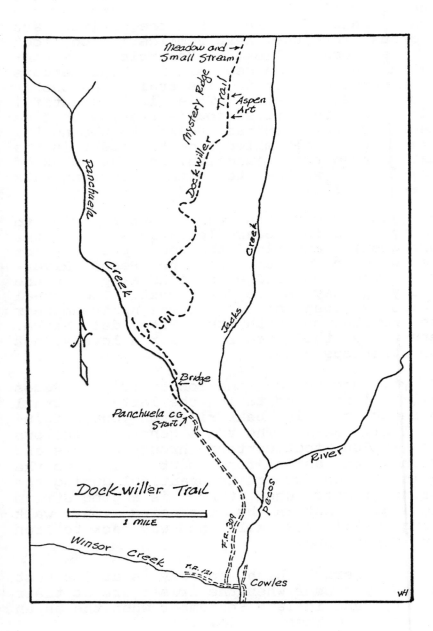

Meadow and
Small Stream

Mystery Ridge Trail

Aspen Art

Panchuela

Dockwiller

Creek

Jacks Creek

Bridge

Panchuela C.G.
Start

Dockwiller Trail

1 MILE

Winsor Creek

River

Pecos

F.R. 309

F.R. 121

Cowles

WH

DOCKWILLER TRAIL

by
Ann Bancroft

U.S. GEOLOGICAL SURVEY MAP REQUIRED: Cowles - 7.5 minute series.

SALIENT FEATURES: Three-season hike. Rife with wildflowers. Wonderful in fall when aspens are turning. This is a little-used trail and although the distant views are not expansive, the wildflowers, aspens, and high, grassy meadows are beautiful and the opportunity for solitude will invite you to linger.

RATING: Moderate.

ROUND TRIP HIKING DISTANCE: 8 miles.

APPROXIMATE HIKING TIME: 5 hours.

ALTITUDE RANGE: Highest point, 10,040 feet; lowest point, 8,350 feet; total vertical ascent, 1,700 feet.

SEASONAL CONSIDERATIONS: Unhikeable in winter. Cool in summer because of dense aspen groves.

ROUND TRIP DRIVING: 91 miles; approximately 3 hours.

DRIVING DIRECTIONS: From Santa Fe drive north on I-25 toward Las Vegas, New Mexico, for approximately 15 miles and exit on the Glorieta off-ramp #299. Turn left on the overpass, then turn right on State Road 50 and drive 6 miles to the town of Pecos. At the stop sign turn left onto State Road 63 which leads north into the Pecos River valley. Measure your mileage from this stop sign. From the Pecos stop sign, drive 20 miles to the road fork where the little settlement of Cowles used to be. Turn left, across the bridge onto Forest Road 121 and after just a few hundred yards turn sharp right uphill on Forest Road 305 toward Los Pinos Ranch and Panchuela Campground. The road dead-ends at Panchuela Campground in about 1 1/2 miles. Park on the right in the large open area reserved for hikers.

HIKING INSTRUCTIONS: From the parking area, walk a short distance upstream to a bridge which spans Panchuela Creek. Cross the bridge and continue hiking upstream along a well-defined trail. A gate will appear; be sure to close it after passing through. About 10 minutes of hiking will bring you to a sign which reads, "Horsethief Meadow 5 1/2; Pecos Baldy Lake 8 1/4; Beatty's Cabin 9." Continue beyond the sign for another 10 minutes until the trail divides. Take the right fork uphill toward Pecos Baldy Lake and Beatty's Cabin. This steeply ascending switchbacked trail is the Dockwiller Trail, named after a man who lived in the Cowles area and ran a sawmill. It is also sometimes referred to as the Mystery Ridge Trail. What the mystery is I haven't been able to discover. The trail takes you uphill out of the Panchuela Creek drainage. In about 40 minutes you may spot the snow cornice between Santa Fe Baldy and Lake Peak toward the west.

After more severe switchbacks, at approximately 9,200 feet, you will begin skirting the Jack's Creek drainage on the flank of Mystery Ridge. Continue along the trail which may sometimes become less well-defined as you pass through grassy areas. Off and on, aspen art may be spotted: words "Dios nos libre. Amen" etched around a cross, or names, possibly of sheepherders, dating as far back as 1919.

After approximately 2 1/2 hours, having taken a leisurely-paced hike with breaks, this hike ends at a large sloping aspen-encircled meadow with a small stream running through it at approximately 10,000 feet. The trail continues on, but for this hike it's time to turn back, retracing your steps to Panchuela Campground.

(This hike leads to many other beautiful areas in the Pecos Wilderness. Someday you may want to go on to Beatty's Cabin or Horsethief Meadow or, if you have someone to do a drive-around, return to Jack's Creek Campground via the Round Mountain trail.)

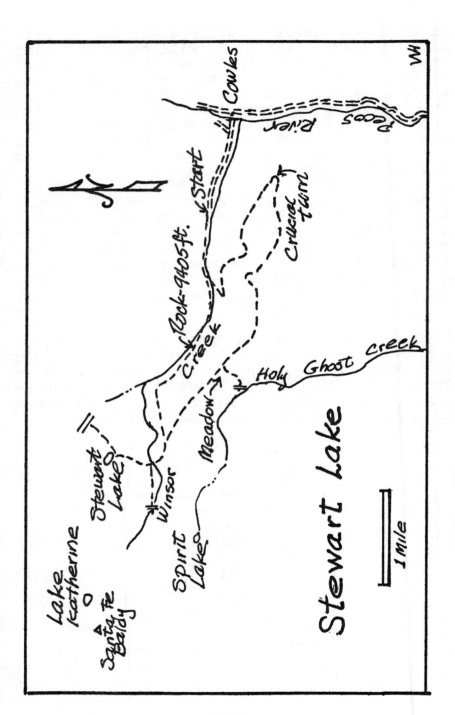

Lake Katherine

Santa Fe Baldy

Stewart Lake

Winsor

Spirit Lake

Stewart Lake

Cowles

Pecos River

Start

Rock-9405ft.

Creek

Critical turn

Holy Ghost creek

Meadow

N

W

1 mile

STEWART LAKE

by
Betsy Fuller and Ann Young

U.S. GEOLOGICAL SURVEY MAP REQUIRED: Cowles 7.5 minute series (the map called "Pecos Wilderness" put out by the National Forest Service is also helpful).

SALIENT FEATURES: The destination is a lovely mountain tarn reached through a deep aspen/conifer forest rife with wildflowers. The return is along a ridge with distant views of the Pecos Wilderness.

RATING: Strenuous.

ROUND TRIP HIKING DISTANCE: 10.5 miles.

APPROXIMATE HIKING TIME: About 6 1/2 hours, including time for breaks and snacks.

ALTITUDE RANGE: Highest point, 10,332 feet; lowest point, 8,400 feet; total vertical ascent, 2,500 feet.

SEASONAL CONSIDERATIONS: Beautiful in the spring as soon as the snow has disappeared and good through the fall until the first heavy snows.

ROUND TRIP DRIVING: 90 miles; 2 hours and 45 minutes.

DRIVING DIRECTIONS: From Santa Fe drive north on I-25 toward Las Vegas, New Mexico,

for approximately 15 miles and exit on the
Glorieta off-ramp #299. Turn left on the
overpass, then turn right on State Road 50
and drive 6 miles to the town of Pecos. At
the stop sign turn left onto State Road 63
which leads north into the Pecos River
valley. Measure your mileage from this stop
sign. From the Pecos stop sign drive 20
miles to the road junction where the little
settlement of Cowles used to be. Turn left
over the bridge onto Forest Road 121 and
continue on for a little over a mile to the
end of the road at Winsor Creek Campground.

HIKING INSTRUCTIONS: From the parking area,
start hiking up the trail that parallels the
creek. You'll be walking through grassy
meadows, aspen glades and wildflower
patches. After about 20 minutes you'll
cross the stream to the left (south) bank
and continue on the well-defined trail still
paralleling the creek just below you.

(About one hundred yards or so after crossing the stream, you'll pass the trail that
you will return on, but it is not marked in
any way and is so obscure that you won't
even notice it unless you know exactly where
to look. Don't worry, it will be clear
coming back.)

The aspens give way to deep conifer forests. You probably will notice a large rock
sticking out part way into the trail with a
U.S.G.S. marker imbedded in it indicating
that the elevation is 9,405 feet. This is a
good place for a break since you will have
been hiking for about an hour by now.

Beyond this point the trail climbs higher
and higher above the stream and finally
you'll lose the sound of it below you.
After about 15 more minutes of climbing

beyond the rock, the trail levels out a little and another 15 minutes will bring you to a trail joining you from the left. Note this junction well because on the return trip you will take the higher trail going back.

For now, though, continue on the trail ahead of you. Shortly - in about 10 minutes more or less of level walking - you will cross a stream over a big log. This is the main fork of the Winsor Creek that you were paralleling down below. A sign here indicates the trail to Lake Katherine but for this hike continue on straight ahead. Another 15 minutes will bring you to Stewart Lake. You'll have to climb up a little rise to get to it. There are many well-worn paths here, so take any one.

This little gem of a lake is spring fed and from the banks of it you can look up to the west and see the flanks of Santa Fe Baldy. Fishermen have made a well-worn path around the lake and after a snack and a rest you may want to walk around it. It won't take more than 15 or 20 minutes with time for admiring the wildflowers included.

To return, take the same path from the lake that you arrived on until you come to the trail junction mentioned previously. You may want to return the way you came but a much more interesting way (although slightly longer by about a mile and a half) is to take the right hand trail that goes along the forested ridge above the trail you came on. (This trail does not show on the Cowles topo map, but if you have the map put out by the Forest Service called "Pecos Wilderness," you'll see it marked.)

In about 20 to 25 minutes from the junction you'll arrive at a meadow with a sign indicating that this is the Pecos Wilderness area. This sign was badly vandalized when I hiked this trail in June of 1989 so if it isn't there or has been replaced by another sign don't worry.

At this point - the very beginning of the meadow - your trail goes off to the left. It's quite faint here. Stay to the left of the meadow for a minute or two until the trail becomes more well defined. (If you find yourself crossing the meadow and dropping down into Holy Ghost Canyon to the right, you've missed your trail. Go back again to the top of the meadow and try again.) The trail is level or very slightly rising and in places where the grass is high becomes a little indistinct, but you should have no trouble finding it. It goes through aspen and then conifer forests and sometimes seems to be following an open swath through the trees. Was this once an ancient sheep-herding trail? You may see an occasional blaze on an old aspen.

In about 35 minutes after you've left the little meadow, an open view will begin to be visible in front of you. This is a nice spot for another break. Continue on the trail for another 20 minutes or so as the trail begins to descend.

Now you come to a place where you have to keep your eyes open because the trail takes a poorly marked sharp turn to the left. (This is about an hour from the trail junction and about 20 minutes from the place where the distant views become visible.) The landmarks to look for are a row of stones placed in a curve to the left, a few large branches to block passage straight

ahead and, to your left, a large old fallen
ponderosa. Go past this ponderosa and the
tall standing stump from which it broke and
you'll quickly find the well defined trail
going down the other side of the ridge
you've been walking on. The trail turns
back on itself toward the left. There may
also be a small rock cairn here marking this
important turn. (If you suddenly find yourself casting about for the trail you have
probably gone a few yards too far ahead.
Back up a little and look for the landmarks
mentioned above.)

From here on there are no problems. Look
off to your right once in a while and you'll
catch glimpses of Pecos Baldy, Round Mountain, Hamilton Mesa and Grass Mountain. The
trail goes down, down, down, seemingly end-
lessly and eventually, after about 45
minutes, you'll hear the stream down below
you and then come to the trail on which you
walked up to the lake. Another 20 minutes
downstream will take you to your car.

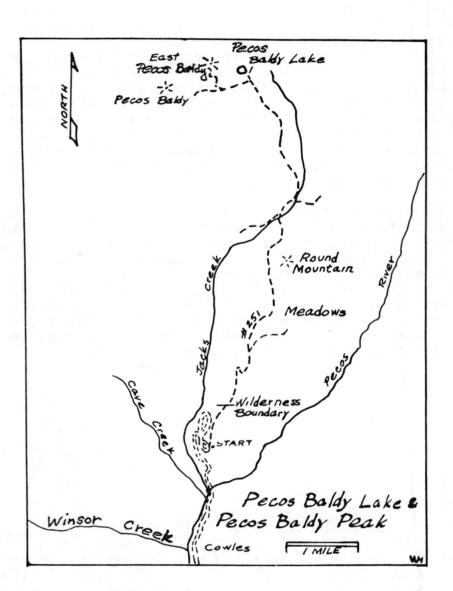

NORTH

East
Pecos Baldy

Pecos
Baldy Lake

Pecos Baldy

Round
Mountain

Creek

River

#251

Meadows

Jacks

Pecos

Cave

Creek

Wilderness
Boundary

START

Pecos Baldy Lake &
Pecos Baldy Peak

Winsor Creek

Cowles

1 MILE

WH

PECOS BALDY LAKE
and
PECOS BALDY PEAK

by
Betsy Fuller

U.S. GEOLOGICAL SURVEY MAPS REQUIRED:
Cowles and Truchas Peak - 7.5 minute series.

SALIENT FEATURES: High country hike, magnificent vistas, wildflowers in summer, high grassy meadows, beautiful mountain lake with possibility of seeing big horn sheep. Allow at least 11 hours round trip from Santa Fe. It's a long drive and a long hike, so get an early start.

RATING: Strenuous.

ROUND TRIP HIKING DISTANCE: 15 miles to Pecos Baldy Lake and 17 miles to East Pecos Baldy Peak.

APPROXIMATE HIKING TIME: 7.5 hours to Pecos Baldy Lake and return, and 9 hours to East Pecos Baldy Peak and return.

ALTITUDE RANGE: For Pecos Baldy Lake: Highest point, 11,320 feet; lowest point, 8,850 feet; total vertical ascent, 2,600 feet. For East Pecos Baldy Peak: Highest point, 12,529 feet; lowest point, 8,850 feet; total vertical ascent, 3,800 feet.

SEASONAL CONSIDERATIONS: A good summer and early fall walk. Probably impassable on foot after the first heavy snow in the fall. Spring flowers late June and July. Fall coloring September and early October.

ROUND TRIP DRIVING: 102 miles - 3.5 hours.

DRIVING DIRECTIONS: From Santa Fe drive north on I-25 toward Las Vegas, New Mexico, for approximately 15 miles and exit on the Glorieta off-ramp #299. Turn left on the overpass, then turn right on State Road 50 and drive 6 miles to the town of Pecos. At the stop sign turn left onto State Road 63 which leads north into the Pecos river valley. Measure your mileage from this stop sign. From the Pecos stop sign drive 20 miles to the road fork where the little settlement of Cowles used to be. Do not take the road to the left which crosses the river, but keep straight ahead for another three miles following the Forest Service signs to Jacks Creek Campground. Keep to the right at every junction until you arrive at a large loop where there are picnic tables, a corral, and parking areas.

HIKING INSTRUCTIONS: The trailhead is to the north of the parking area where there is a Forest Service sign. The trail starts with a long climb (about a mile) through a conifer forest up the side of a hill. During this climb you will enter the Pecos Wilderness. Soon after the initial long climb, the trail goes into a series of long switchbacks still rising, until finally, after about another mile the trail levels off a little. Just after another short climb, you will reach an open sloping grassy area. At this point, there is a signpost marking a three-way trail junction. You will have walked about 2.5 miles and climbed about 1,050 feet. Your altitude here is 10,026 feet.

Take the left (north) fork of the trail and continue through the meadow toward the aspen trees. After passing through the aspens, the trail swings slightly to the right. Watch for beautiful distant views of the Pecos Valley to the east and the mountains to the west as you look all around you. The trail climbs up through an open meadow in a northerly direction. At the northern end of this meadow the trail enters a conifer forest and drops down to Jack's Creek which is shallow most of the year and can easily be crossed by stepping stones. At this point you will have walked another 2 miles in about 45 minutes to an hour.

Cross Jack's Creek, follow the trail to the right paralleling the stream. In 5 minutes, the trail swings away from the stream. In 15 minutes after crossing Jack's Creek, the trail splits. Go straight ahead to Pecos Baldy, not right to Beatty's Cabin. Continue climbing through deep and dark conifer forests. Your altitude here is now over 10,500 feet and the trail is steep in some places, so take it easy as you continue your ascent. Finally, about 2 miles (and over an hour's walking) after you crossed Jack's Creek, you will leave the forest behind you and will see the summit of East Baldy Peak ahead of you. One last steep climb brings you out at yet another junction from which point you will see Pecos Baldy Lake just a few hundred feet away.

If you're tired (and you will be!) go down to the lake for a snack and a rest. As you're recovering from the steep walk, search the sides of the mountain for bighorn sheep which are often found here in the summer months. Sometimes the ewes and the lambs are overfriendly, nuzzling into your knapsack if it's left unattended. It will make a great picture, though, if you have a camera handy.

You may want to end the outward bound trip here and return back over the same route. If you've still got enough energy left to climb to the top of East Pecos Baldy, rising above you (1100 feet up), go back up the couple of hundred feet to the place where you first saw the lake and where there is a marker prohibiting camping in the lake basin. Take the trail to the southwest (to your right as you walk away from the lake) and follow it for about 1/2 a mile until it comes out into an open saddle. Don't take the trail to the left that goes downhill through the woods, but continue across the open saddle in the same general direction that you were following when you arrived. You will have no trouble finding the rocky path that now zigzags up the steep side of the mountain. The climb from the saddle to the top of East Pecos Baldy is another 680 feet and a hard pull at this elevation (12,529 feet when you reach the top), so take your time and enjoy the ever enlarging views as you climb to the top. Don't attempt this part of the hike if it's stormy. There's no protection on top, and lightning and strong winds are not good companions when you're on the top of a bare rocky peak in the high mountains. There is frequently a snow cornice along the peak, with a considerable overhang. Do not walk out on any snow field along the edge of the peak.

Your return trip is over the same route as the one you came on, the only difference (an important one!) being that you'll be going downhill most of the time.

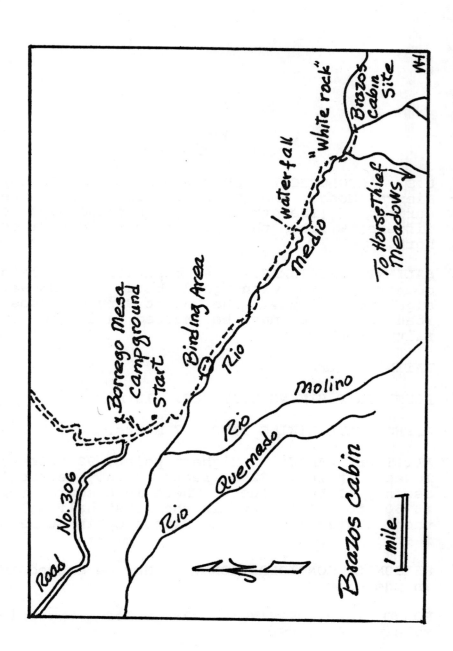

Road No. 306

x Borrego Mesa campground
Start

Binding Area

Rio

Rio Medio

waterfall

"white rock"

Brazos Cabin Site

To HorseThief Meadows ↓

Rio Molino

Rio Quemado

Brazos Cabin

1 mile

BRAZOS CABIN

by
John O. Baxter

U.S. GEOLOGICAL SURVEY MAPS REQUIRED: Sierra Mosca and Truchas Peak - 7.5 minute series. (The trail shown on these maps is different from the current trail described here.)

SALIENT FEATURES: A beautiful mountain country hike with good bird and flower sightings likely. The Forest Service access road No. 306 may be rutted and muddy in rainy weather.

RATING: Strenuous.

ROUND TRIP HIKING DISTANCE: 12 miles.

APPROXIMATE HIKING TIME: 7 hours.

ALTITUDE RANGE: Highest point, 9200 feet; lowest point, 8250 feet; total vertical ascent, 1550 feet. There is a sharp drop (8850 to 8250 feet) in the first half mile, then a gradual climb to Brazos Cabin at 9200 feet.

SEASONAL CONSIDERATIONS: May be snowed in in the winter.

ROUND TRIP DRIVING: 78 miles - approximately 2.5 hours.

DRIVING DIRECTIONS: Take the Taos Highway, U.S. #84-285, north from Santa Fe 16 miles to the Nambé turnoff. Turn right on N.M. 503. Note the odometer reading at this turn. At the Cundiyo-Chimayo junction, avoid the left turn to Chimayo. Continue straight ahead toward Cundiyo and Santa Cruz Lake. After driving 13.5 miles from the Nambé turnoff, where you took your odometer reading, turn right on Forest Service Road #306 and continue 9 miles to the entrance to Borrego Mesa Campground. Turn right once more on FS #435. The trailhead is a half mile from the entrance, with parking available both within the camp ground and along the road. The last 5 miles of this drive can become slippery in rainy weather.

HIKING INSTRUCTIONS: A Forest Service sign marked "Rio Medio" indicates the beginning of your route. The trail sets off in an easterly direction, rising slightly for about 100 yards before plunging sharply downward into Rio Medio Canyon. On the right, the green silhouette of Sierra Mosca looms over the valley to the south. Winding through towering ponderosas and patches of oak, the trail makes a descent of 600 feet in the first half mile, leading to the clear waters of the Rio Medio. Don't forget that this same steep slope must be negotiated in reverse at the end of the hike when the scenery may seem less remarkable.

Continuing eastward, the track follows the north bank of the river upstream. Birders should find several mountain species in this area such as Steller's Jays, Hairy Woodpeckers and Western Wood Peewees. Broadtailed Hummingbirds are often seen feeding at the scarlet penstemon blossoms which border the trail. Unfortunately the canyon is also the home of some of New Mexico's most belligerent insects including clouds of voracious gnats in June and equally hungry deer flies later on. THAT'S why they call it Sierra Mosca! (Fly Mountain).

After proceeding up the Rio Medio approximately 1.5 miles, you will come to the first of two crossings, about half a mile apart. Made of whatever logs and branches are available, these impromptu bridges wash out each spring so that their degree of stability following reconstruction is unpredictable. If you find that a high wire act is unappealing, it is possible to avoid crossing altogether by bushwhacking along the north bank. Once past these obstacles, the trail gradually climbs the side of the canyon for 2 miles, making several swings away from the river to cross a series of arroyos which come down from the north. In the largest of these, a small waterfall gurgles cheerfully among moss and ferns. If a snack now seems in order, reward yourself with the tiny raspberries which grow in profusion nearby as the trail returns to the Medio. At this point a large boulder protrudes over the rushing stream, which older hikers will instantly recognize as the perch of the White Rock nymph, one of the classic advertising symbols of an earlier era. Chances of seeing the maiden herself are less certain.

Because the canyon is much narrower here, the trail is forced close to the creek and it is necessary to clamber along the face of sheer granite cliffs in a few places. After making an easy crossing on a huge ponderosa, the track makes its way through a heavy log drift fence where it divides. The right fork heads up the divide towards Horsethief

Meadows in the Pecos drainage and the head-
waters of the Rio Frijoles. Take the left
fork on up the canyon for another mile and
you will come to a large meadow, the site of
Brazos Cabin. The cabin itself is no longer
there. In this part of the valley, which
opens rather suddenly, there are many
pleasant locations to enjoy your lunch and
the beauty of the Sangre de Cristos before
retracing your footsteps towards the
trailhead.

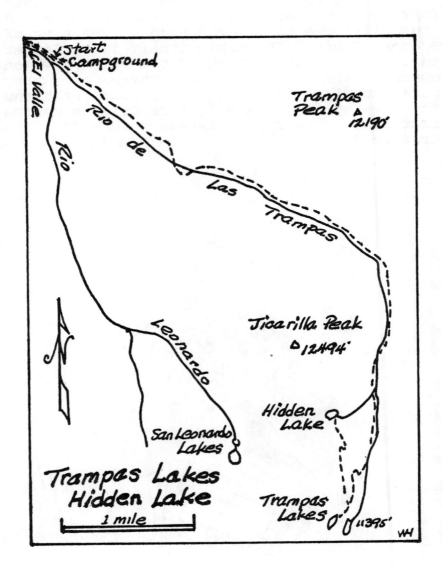

Start
Campground

El Valle

Rio de Las Trampas

Rio

Trampas
Peak △
12190'

Jicarilla Peak
△ 12494'

Leonardo

Hidden
Lake

San Leonardo
Lakes

Trampas Lakes
Hidden Lake

1 mile

Trampas
Lakes
11395'

WH

-98-

TRAMPAS LAKES/HIDDEN LAKE

by
Betsy Fuller

U.S. GEOLOGICAL SURVEY MAPS REQUIRED: El Valle and Truchas Peak - 7.5 minute series.

SALIENT FEATURES: Good trail through deep coniferous forests, much of the time above a clear fast running stream.   Lovely hidden lakes surrounded by towering peaks. Wildflowers in season.

RATING: Strenuous.

ROUND TRIP HIKING DISTANCE: 11.5 miles to Trampas Lakes.   Extension to Hidden Lake, 2 miles additional.

APPROXIMATE HIKING TIME: 6 hours to Trampas Lakes.   Additional 1.5 hours for Hidden Lake extension.

ALTITUDE RANGE: Highest point, 11,395 feet; lowest point, 8960 feet; total vertical ascent to Trampas Lakes, 2440 feet, and to Hidden Lake, 2700 feet.

SEASONAL CONSIDERATIONS: A late spring, summer, and early fall walk.

ROUND TRIP DRIVING: Approximately 108 miles in about 3 to 4 hours.

DRIVING DIRECTIONS: Take US 285 north out of Santa Fe for approximately 16 miles from the plaza past the turn-off to Los Alamos (State Road 502) and continue on for about 0.5 miles over a slight rise and down to the Nambé River (usually a sandy wash here). Just after crossing the bridge over this river, turn right (east) on State Road 503 toward Chimayo. After about 7.5 miles from the turn-off onto State Road 503, take a left turn (north) unto State Road 520 to Chimayo. Go through the little settlement of Chimayo until you come to the junction with State Road 76. Turn right (east) on State Road 76 toward Truchas. After about 7.7 miles from this junction and just as you get into the settled part of the village of Truchas, #76 takes a sharp turn to the left (north). The turn here is between two buildings and hardly looks like a main thoroughfare but there is a sign here showing that the road goes to Peñasco and Picuris. It may also be identified as the High Road to Taos.

Take a new odometer reading and continue on #76 through the villages of Ojo Sarco and Las Trampas. Soon after you pass through the village of Las Trampas, be sure to notice the old log flume on the right, still carrying water from the higher elevations over the ravine to the irrigation ditches of the village below. In about 8.7 miles from Truchas and about a mile beyond Trampas, you come to Forest Service Road #207 (sometimes unmarked) going off to the right (east). Take this road and drive past the settlement of El Valle to the very end of FS #207, about 8.1 miles. The road ends at a primitive campground. Park here.

HIKING INSTRUCTIONS: Now you can get a close look at the Rio de las Trampas whose course you have been following in the car.

It comes rushing out of a rather deep little canyon, probably the reason the road comes to an end here.

The trail is up about 20 feet on the hill to your left as you face up the river. After this initial clamber, the trail starts its steady upward path. You are at about 8960 feet here and you have about 2400 feet to climb to the lakes in about 5 miles. You will pass through a gate (be sure to close it behind you) and after about 45 minutes the trail will cross to the south side of the stream and then again to the north side. This is where a snow avalanche came down the side of the mountain a few years ago taking all the trees down with it. The area is now regenerating into a lovely open meadow usually filled with a kaleidoscope of wildflowers.

Until you get very near the lakes, you will be walking along the left side of the river, most of the time quite far above it, but within earshot of it and with occasional glimpses of it rushing below you. There are several long switchbacks that help ease your way up, and finally, several crossings of the river which, except during the spring snow melt, should be no problem. Fallen tree trunks and stepping stones can be useful in crossing.

At the right time of year, usually early to mid-July, you find unbelievably beautiful gardens of marsh marigolds, brook cress, false hellebore, wild candytuft, thimble-berry, cranesbill, osha, cow parsnip, Parry's primrose and many, many other flowers. Look back down the valley once in a while and you will catch glimpses of the flat land around Española way below you in the Rio Grande valley. The views are not expansive, but it will give you a good idea of how high up you are.

Finally you will "top out" at a level, sometimes marshy, area. Although you cannot see the lakes from here, there should be a sign identifying them and a walk of a few hundred yards straight ahead will bring you to them. They are separated from each other by a low ridge and both provide beautiful sites for lunch and photographs.

EXTENSION: From these lakes you can either return directly to your car down the trail over which you have just come or you can take an extension to Hidden Lake. This extension will consume about 1.5 hours including time for a snack at the lake and will add about 2 miles to the total distance.

If you want to go on to Hidden Lake, return to the place where you topped out, and where the sign identifying Trampas Lakes is. Then, instead of going back down the steep trail you came up, bear to your left. You will be walking along a good trail that is almost parallel with the trail you came on, but above it. Gradually the trail to Hidden Lake will bear off to the left, and after a couple of mild switchbacks, you will descend to the lake itself. You will have dropped about 280 feet from the Trampas Lakes to Hidden Lake, and you will now have to climb back up in order to start the return trek home. The return trip to your car is over the same trail on which you walked to get to the lakes. Tighten your boot laces because it's downhill all the way!

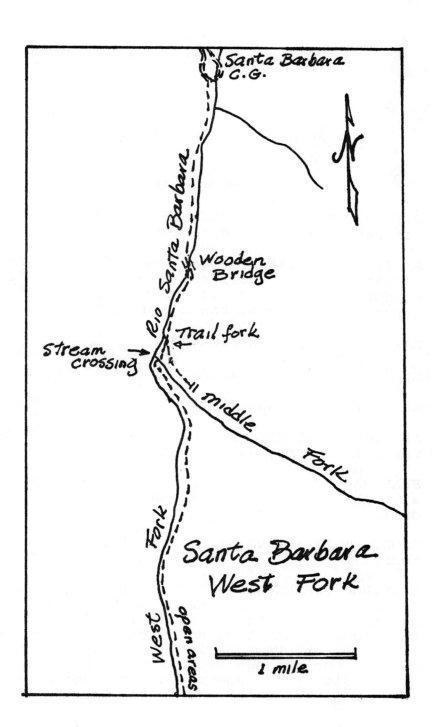

Santa Barbara C.G.

N

Rio Santa Barbara

Wooden Bridge

Trail fork

Stream crossing

Middle

Fork

Fork

Santa Barbara West Fork

West

open areas

1 mile

SANTA BARBARA WEST FORK

by
Linda and John Buchser

U.S. GEOLOGICAL SURVEY MAP REQUIRED: Jicarita Peak - 7.5 minute series.

SALIENT FEATURES: The west fork of Santa Barbara Creek provides a transition from meadows and aspen forest to alpine tundra, depending on the distance you travel.

RATING: Easy to strenuous.

ROUND TRIP HIKING DISTANCE: 6 - 12 miles.

APPROXIMATE HIKING TIME: 3 1/2 to 7 hours.

ALTITUDE RANGE: 8,868 to 9,880 feet; total vertical ascent, 1,100 feet.

SEASONAL CONSIDERATIONS: Road closed several miles before Santa Barbara campground during snow season.

ROUND TRIP DRIVING: 143 miles; 2 1/2 - 3 hours.

DRIVING DIRECTIONS: From Santa Fe take US 84/285 north to Española. In Española, stay on the main street as US 84/285 go off to the left. Continuing straight ahead you will be on New Mexico 68 headed toward Taos. Go through Velarde and along the Rio Grande to Embudo where you turn right (east) onto New Mexico 75. Continue through Dixon and Peñasco.   When you come toward the end of Peñasco, Highway 75 turns sharply left (toward Vadito).   Don't take this left turn.   Keep on going straight ahead toward Rodarte.   After about 1.5 miles, the road you are on will turn right. Just before you come to this turn, look for a dirt road that goes off to the left. This is your road, Forest Service Road 116. There might be a brown Forest Service sign directing you to Santa Barbara campground. Follow this dirt road for six miles to Santa Barbara campground.

HIKING   INSTRUCTIONS: Park in the area before the cattle guard entrance to the campground, and hike through the campground on either the upper or lower road.

Beginning   at the southern end of Santa Barbara campground, the foot trail passes through a fence and crosses a small feeder stream prior to joining the main horse trail.   At about one mile, the trail is rerouted to avoid a washed out area and ascends through an aspen stand. Looking down from this higher portion, one can see a beaver lodge and a dam on a side area of the creek.   Later, the trail runs along the main flow of Santa Barbara Creek.

In a normally wet year there is a continuous show of wildflowers from April through September, and a great variety, since the changes in habitat and elevation provide a wide range of growing conditions. At about 1.6 miles, there is a wooden bridge crossing the creek. This first section of trail, and return, is an easy day hike for those with small children or small energies. Now the trail increases its rate of ascent.   At about 2.3 miles you will see a sign indicating the fork which would take you on up trail number 24, to the middle and the east forks of Santa Barbara Creek. Continue up the west fork, trail number 25; in another .2 mile there is a stream crossing which has a number of peeled logs jammed across as a make-shift foot way.

(If it is the rainy season, you may find these logs dry enough to cross on the way in, but under water on the way out. In this case, the creek may be forded just upstream of the logs, but use caution in the swift water and expect to get wet up to your hips. During the spring runoff, the stream may be too deep to ford at all.)

The stream you have just crossed is actually a combination of the east and middle forks and you are now between them and the west fork, which is out of sight at this point. The trail moves higher on the mountainside, and though the west fork is now often visible, access to it is down inconveniently steep and loose slopes.

At about mile 4.7, you come out of the trees and pass through open areas. On the stream below are more beaver dams. These intermittent meadows continue to the end of the valley. Cattle grazing is permitted here only in the fall of every third year, so meadow wildflowers can be magnificent when there has been sufficient rain. Chimayosos Mountain comes into view spectacularly to the south. One reaches the end of the meadows at about mile 6, with a sign indicating another 6 miles to the divide. The trail goes on up to the Divide but this is the turn-around point for this hike.

Return by the same route.

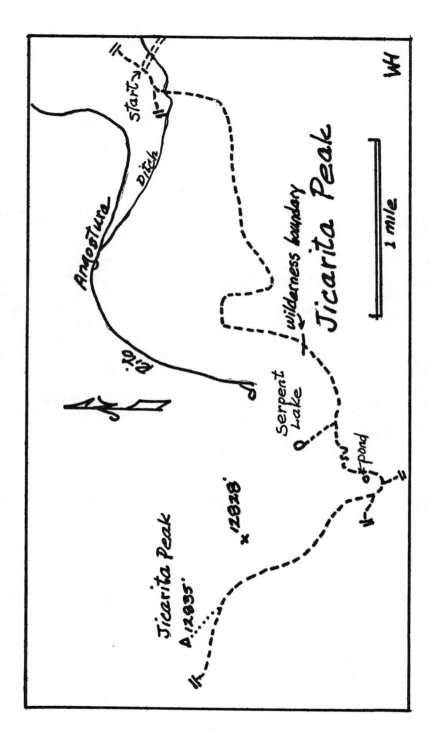

JICARITA PEAK

by
Norma McCallan

U.S. GEOLOGICAL SURVEY MAP REQUIRED: Jicarita Peak - 7.5 minute series.

SALIENT FEATURES: This hike to the tenth highest peak in New Mexico affords marvelous vistas of the surrounding countryside, incredible displays of alpine wildflowers, and a sense of being on the very top of the world. The peak itself is easily climbed, and can be done as a day hike. Because the peak and its approach are well above timberline, caution is urged in the event of approaching storms. Frequent thunderstorms play around the Santa Barbara Divide in the summer, and that exposed terrain is not the place to be when lightning is striking.

RATING: Strenuous.

ROUND TRIP HIKING DISTANCE: Approximately 11 miles.

APPROXIMATE HIKING TIME: 6 to 9 hours.

ALTITUDE RANGE: Highest point, 12,835 feet; lowest point, 10,400; total vertical ascent, 2,435 feet.

SEASONAL CONSIDERATIONS: June to October would be best; earlier or later one may run into snow, and even June or October could be

risky.   The   dirt   road to the trailhead is
not plowed in the winter.

ROUND TRIP DRIVING: 151 miles; 4 hours.

DRIVING   DIRECTIONS: Take US 285 north out
of   Santa   Fe for approximately 16 miles from
the   plaza   past   the   turn-off to Los Alamos
(State   Road   502)   and continue on for about
0.5   miles over a slight rise and down to the
Nambé   River   (usually   a   sandy   wash here).
Just   after   crossing   the   bridge   over this
river,   turn   right   (east) on State Road 503
toward   Chimayo.   After about 7.5 miles from
the   turn-off   onto   State   Road   503, take a
left   turn   (north)   unto   State   Road 520 to
Chimayo.   Go   through the little settlement
of   Chimayo   until   you   come to the junction
with   State   Road   76.   Turn right (east) on
State   Road   76   toward Truchas. After about
7.7   miles   and   just   as   you   get   into the
settled   part   of the village of Truchas, #76
takes   a   sharp   turn to the left (north). The
turn   here   is   between   two   buildings   and
hardly   looks   like   a   main thoroughfare but
there   is   a   sign here showing that the road
goes   to Peñasco and Picuris. It may also be
identified   as the High Road to Taos.   Take a
new   odometer   reading   and   continue   on #76
through   the   villages   of   Ojo Sarco and Las
Trampas.   Turn right onto state Road 75 just
before   the   village   of Peñasco and continue
through   Peñasco.   At   the   end of Peñasco,
turn   left,   still   on   #75,   through Vadito.
When   you   dead   end   in   ten   minutes   from
Peñsaco   at a T intersection, turn right onto
State   Road   518.   This   road   goes   past a
number   of   Forest   Service   campgrounds   and
through   the   small village of Tres Ritos.   At
1.7   miles   past Angostura Camp turn right
onto   Forest   Service Road #161. You can see
the   Forest   Service   road marker a few yards

in on the right hand side of the dirt road. Stay on this road until it dead ends at 4.6 miles and park.

HIKING INSTRUCTIONS: At the spot you have parked you will notice a Forest Service marker identifying the trail as Santa Barbara-Angostura Trail #18, and showing that Angostura Campground is to be reached on the small trail going right, while the main trail goes to Alamitos Road. Go left (straight) on what is really an extension of the road you drove in on. Within a quarter mile or so you will see another Forest Service sign saying Serpent Lake Trail #19, and indicating that the right fork of the trail goes to Agua Piedra, 7 miles, while the left fork goes to Serpent Lake, 3 miles. Take this left fork. Only a few yards further you will come to another intersection, with a blue arrow and the National Recreational Trail insignia on the fork which branches right, and a single blue arrow and insignia on a tree straight ahead. Stay straight, and mark this intersection in your mind so that when you return you will not make the mistake of following the blue arrows onto what will then be a left-hand turn. Very shortly you will cross a fast-flowing ditch; there should be enough stones and logs to make a relatively easy crossing. The trail continues through the forest, going upward at a comfortable incline. About 1 1/2 miles in you will pass a series of meadows on the left, which make a good spot for a rest stop.

At about 2 1/2 miles you will come to a boundary sign for the Pecos Wilderness. Soon thereafter, as you turn a corner, you will see the stark outline of the Santa Barbara Divide through the trees. About a half mile further you will come to the intersection of the Serpent Lake Trail, heading off to the right, while the main trail has a sign showing that it is 11 miles further to Santa Barbara Campground and 10 miles back to Agua Piedra Campground. Serpent Lake is only about a quarter mile down the side trail.

Continuing up the main trail after the Serpent Lake intersection you will soon come out of the forest and start switchbacks up through the scree and through isolated clumps of stunted spruce and bristlecone pine. As you go higher these pygmy forests will be replaced by dense patches of willow, and everywhere in the scree will be magnificent bouquets of alpine flowers. Just before you get to the top of the Divide you will pass a small pond on the right.

Once on top you will find an old sign pointing back down the trail with the barely legible legend that Serpent Lake is 2 miles and Agua Piedra Campground is also that way. A few feet further stands a post where a newer sign used to be, showing the Santa Barbara Campground to be 9 miles. Do not continue any further on this Angostura Trail, which meanders over the ridge and switchbacks down to the Middle Fork of the Santa Barbara River, even though it will have the more prominent cairns and better worn path. Instead, while standing by the sign, look to your right, and you will see a series of smaller cairns and patches of trail heading northwest. Follow these cairns as the trail contours along the ridge near the top of the Divide and detours around the south side of a large unnamed 12,828 foot peak. In some stretches, alternate trails and cairns exist - don't worry, they all seem to end up in the same place.

Not until you are well around this peak will Jicarita Peak itself be visible - its flat top and trapezoidal shape suddenly dominating the horizon in front of you. Stay on this small trail until you reach the closest corner of Jicarita. The trail itself contours around the south and west sides of Jicarita and meets the trail coming up from Indian Creek at the northwest corner of Jicarita. Get off the trail and walk up the southeast corner of Jicarita. If you watch closely you will find patches of trail going up through the scree and grass of the slope. Soon you will be on the flat, wide top, with vistas in all directions, and several rock shelters if you want to eat your lunch out of the ever present wind. The southern horizon is particularly awesome, with the jagged Truchas Peaks and the gentler slopes of Trampas and Chimayosos Peaks dominating the skyline. Always observe caution when up on the Divide and watch for storm clouds; summer thunderstorms can roll in fast and you do not want to be above timberline when the lightning starts striking.

Return the way you came.

Note: If you should want to make this into a backpack, Serpent Lake is an ideal campsite half way up the trail. It is situated in a lovely grassy meadow and you can set your tent up in the dwarfed trees just north of the lake, then proceed on up to Jicarita Peak, and return the next day. I do not know why the lake got its name, other than several little grassy hummocks in the lake look rather like a small serpent swimming along, when viewed from the trail above.

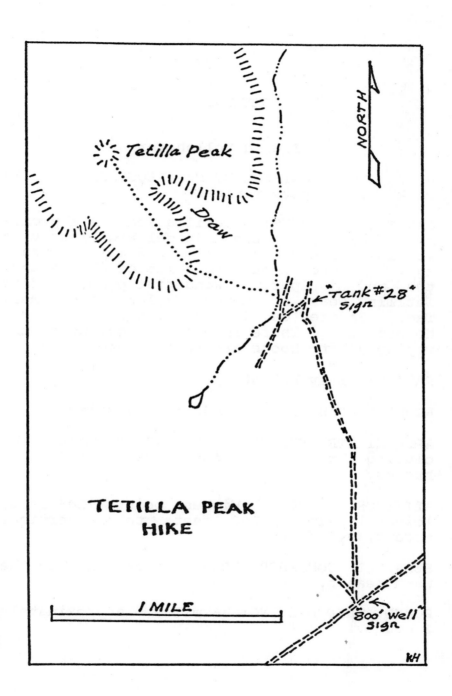

NORTH

Tetilla Peak

Draw

"Tank #28" Sign

"800' Well" Sign

TETILLA PEAK
HIKE

1 MILE

kH

TETILLA PEAK

by
Ingrid Vollnhofer

U.S. GEOLOGICAL SURVEY MAP REQUIRED: Tetilla Peak - 7.5 minute series.

SALIENT FEATURES: Tetilla Peak is a prominent volcano on the Caja del Rio Plateau, a volcanic field formed some 2.6 million years ago. An open area with a lot of cholla cactus and juniper. Wonderful panorama from Tetilla Peak of Mount Taylor, the Jemez, Taos, Sangre de Cristo, Ortiz, and Sandia Mountains. There is a lot of cactus on the way so hiking boots are recommended.

RATING: Easy but steep.

ROUND TRIP HIKING DISTANCE: 2.5 miles.

APPROXIMATE HIKING TIME: 2 to 3 hours including breathing, vista, water and snack breaks.

ALTITUDE RANGE: Highest point, 7206 feet; lowest point, 6260 feet; total vertical ascent, 946 feet.

SEASONAL CONSIDERATIONS: Pretty hot in the warm season.

ROUND TRIP DRIVING: 36 miles - approximately 2 hours.

DRIVING DIRECTIONS: Take Cerrillos Road south. Turn right onto Airport Road. Measure your mileage from this turn. Pass the golf course. At 2.7 miles swing right at the "Y." There is a small sign, "Forest Bdy. 9." Continue past the sewage disposal plant, and the Santa Fe Polo Grounds. At 6.4 miles, turn right. This graded dirt road crosses a cattle guard, then climbs the hill to the left. At the top (7.6 miles), when the road turns sharply to the right, you drive straight ahead onto a rough, primitive road. (For a good winter strenuous hike, you can park here, walk the power line and head for Tetilla Peak. This is about 12 miles round trip.) This stretch of the road to the gate is the roughest; rocky and rutty. My little Honda Civic did fine, though. The road can be muddy and can become impassable in wet snows and rain.

About a quarter of a mile after you drive onto the small dirt road, a branch road takes off to the right, in the direction of the power line. Ignore it. Ignore all various turnouts and continue on the obvious road. You come to a "Y" and you can continue straight but it is very rutty. It is better to swing left around this rutty dip. At 8.4 miles you come to a gate. Please close it behind you. You go through one cattle guard after this. At 12.1 miles you come to a fence line and a sign that says "800 well, Santa Fe 21, Trail 24." Turn right here. At 13.5 miles, the road splits. Turn left at the "Tank #28" sign and park.

HIKING INSTRUCTIONS: There is no trail. This walk is a free-for-all. Head for Tetilla Peak in front of you. There is no other peak around. Avoid the draw, which you see at first. Keep to the left of it and stay high. While climbing, look back

and note some distant high landmark in the
direction of your car to guide you on the
way down. It is easier to go off course
than this open landscape would lead you to
believe. At the very last stretch, the walk
is quite steep, almost a scramble. Don't
forget, the view at the top is magnificent.

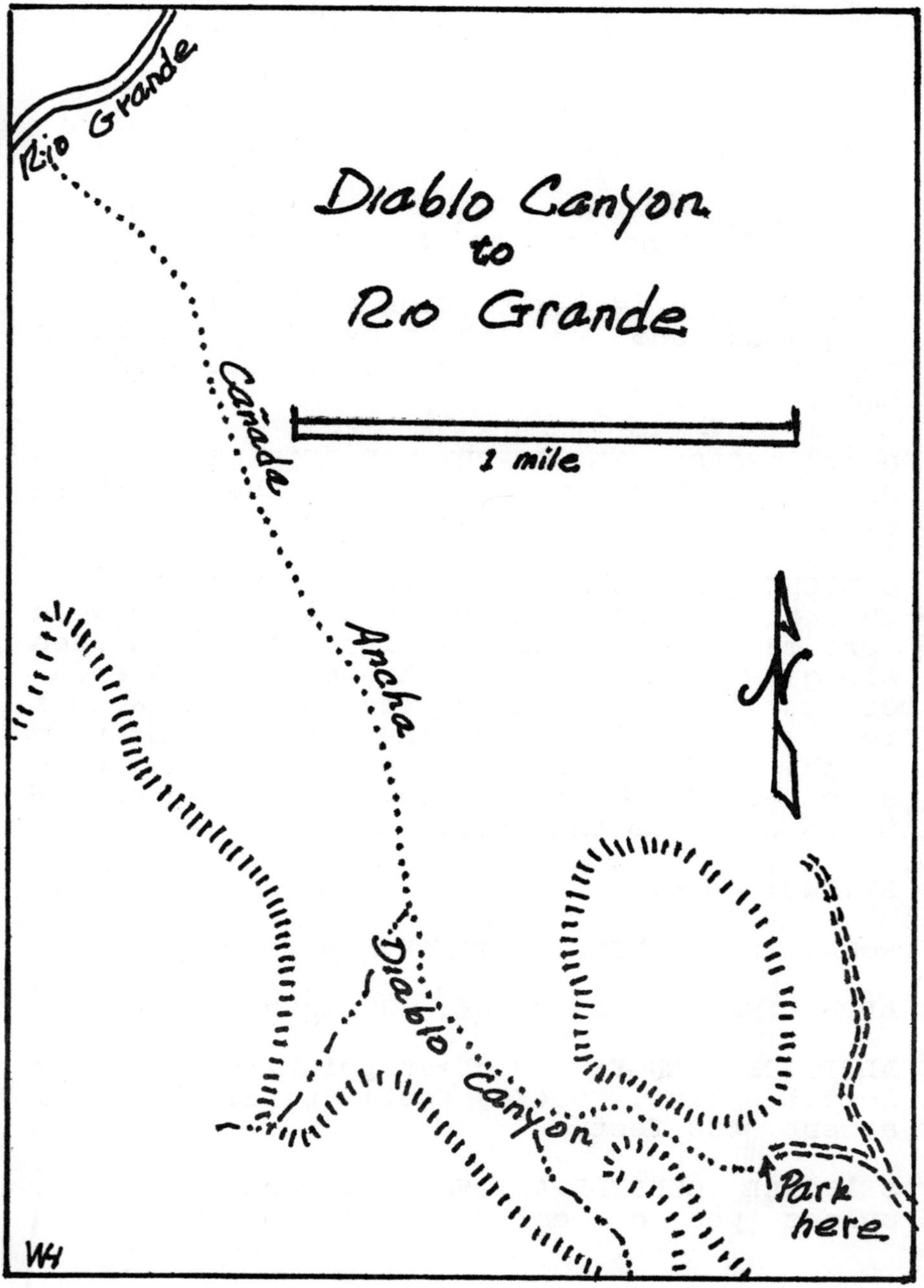

Diablo Canyon
to
Rio Grande

Rio Grande

Cañada

Ancha

Diablo Canyon

1 mile

N

Park
here

WH

DIABLO CANYON TO RIO GRANDE

by
Polly Robertson and Norbert Sperlich

Note: This is a variation of the hike first suggested and written up by Polly Robertson for the first and second editions of the book.

U.S. GEOLOGICAL SURVEY MAP REQUIRED: White Rock - 7.5 minute series. On the map, Diablo Canyon is called Caja del Rio Canyon.

SALIENT FEATURES: This hike takes you through a short but spectacular canyon with vertical walls of basalt, and continues along a sandy arroyo to the Rio Grande. Great views all along the way. The access road is poorly maintained and can be very rough. Four-wheel drive and a high clearance are a great advantage when road conditions are less than perfect.

RATING: Easy.

ROUND TRIP HIKING DISTANCE: 6 miles.

APPROXIMATE HIKING TIME: 3 hours.

ALTITUDE RANGE: Highest point, 5,850 feet; lowest point, 5,450 feet; total vertical ascent, 400 feet.

SEASONAL CONSIDERATIONS: Too hot in summer, unless you go early in the morning. Road may not be passable after heavy rain or snow.

ROUND TRIP DRIVING: About 36 miles - 1 hour and 40 minutes or longer depending on road conditions.

DRIVING DIRECTIONS: Take Washington Avenue north from the plaza. Turn left in front of the pink-stuccoed Scottish Rite Temple onto Paseo de Peralta. At the intersection with Guadalupe Street, turn right and follow Guadalupe, which joins Highway 84/285. Continue north on Highway 84/285 to Camino de la Tierra on your left just past the median wall. This is about 2.5 miles from the plaza. Turn left onto Camino de la Tierra. Take your mileage at the turnoff. You will be driving on this road (which becomes Buckman Road after a while) for about 15.5 miles. The first 5.5 miles are paved and take you to the La Tierra development. Occasionally, the road splits, and there will be trees and bushes separating the two lanes. Stay on the right lane and go straight ahead at intersections. Once you come to the unpaved part of the road, you will encounter washboard surface, cattle guards, and ruts or deep sand where the road is crossed by drainages. Slow down!

About 11 miles from the turnoff onto La Tierra Road you will pass a windmill (Dead Dog Well) and a corral on your left. Take a mileage reading here. At this point a wide arroyo (Cañada Ancha) comes in from the left. This arroyo follows the edge of the Caja del Rio volcanic field. The latter is now visible on your left, forming a basalt-capped escarpment. The road stays to the right of the escarpment, going downhill over sandy terrain. Soon, the vertical cliffs of

Diablo Canyon will appear ahead of you to the left. The canyon separates a small mesa that is edged by basalt cliffs from the lava mesa to the west. At 4.3 miles from the windmill look for a secondary road that branches off to the left and toward Diablo Canyon. Take this road to an open area close to the mouth of the canyon. Park your car here.

HIKING INSTRUCTIONS: Head toward the arroyo that goes into the canyon. You will have to cross a fence. As you enter the canyon, you will have vertical basalt cliffs on your right, rising up some 300 feet. As you go deeper into the canyon, you will notice that the basalt columns rest on sand and gravel. A very unstable foundation, indeed. About ten minutes into the hike, you will come to a place where water is seeping out of the ground. To the right of this spot, where basalt columns form an overhang, cliff swallows like to build their nests. In the summertime, you can see swallows feeding their young. The unique descending scale call of the canyon wren can often be heard here. Soon, the canyon widens and, on your right and toward the top of the mesa, basalt cliffs give way to layers of ashes and cinders that have been eroded into jagged shapes.

As you walk out of the canyon, the arroyo widens and heads north for a while, toward Buckman Mesa. The arroyo soon swerves left (northwest) and descends slowly toward the Rio Grande. If you look skyward once in a while, you may see hawks or ravens circling above. Ahead of you, on the other side of the (still hidden) Rio Grande, you will see dark basalt cliffs topped by orange tuff. The basalt comes from the Caja del Rio volcanoes; the tuff was produced by eruptions of the Jemez caldera. After hiking a little over an hour, you will come to the river. From this point look upstream toward Buckman Mesa and its small peak. Does it look like a hound dog or a crocodile in profile? Had you been here around the turn of the century, you would have encountered a bridge crossing the river, a railroad line, and a settlement built by lumberman Henry Buckman. It's all gone now. The Buckman area is important for Santa Fe, however, because here are wells that produce part of the water supply.

Return to your car the way you came. Yes, it is hotter now, you are going uphill, and walking in the sand seems to be more tiresome. But once again you will enter Diablo Canyon and find a shady spot to linger a while, before you drive back to Santa Fe.

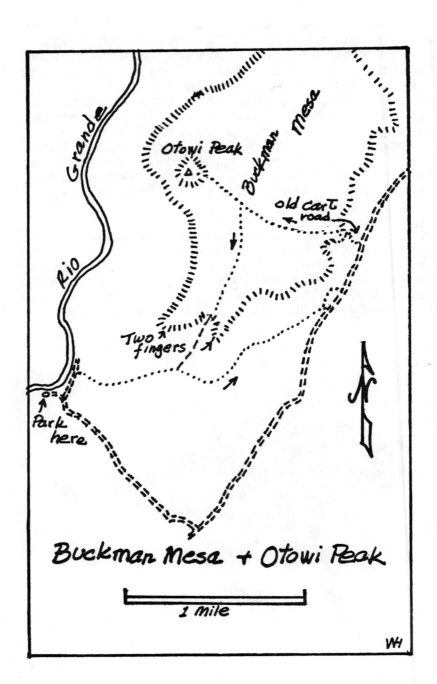

Grande

Rio

Otowi Peak

Buckman Mesa

old cart road

Two fingers

Park here

Buckman Mesa + Otowi Peak

1 mile

WH

BUCKMAN MESA AND OTOWI PEAK

by
Polly Robertson and Norbert Sperlich

Note: This is a variation of the hike first suggested and written up by Polly Robertson for the first and second editions of this book.

U.S. GEOLOGICAL SURVEY MAP REQUIRED: White Rock - 7.5 minute series.

SALIENT FEATURES: Buckman Mesa is the isolated mesa south of Otowi Bridge that guards the entrance to White Rock Canyon. Most of the mesa top is flat except for its western corner, where Otowi Peak, the remnant of a volcano, rises 1,100 feet above the Rio Grande. The peak offers magnificent views in all directions.

Most of the hike goes over rough terrain. There are no trails on top of the mesa. Only experienced hikers who know how to use topo map and compass should attempt this hike! The access road can be very rough, rutted and/or muddy, especially after rain or snow. Four-wheel drive and a high clearance are a great advantage when road conditions are less than perfect. Bring water.

RATING: Moderate in distance. People not used to off-trail hiking may find this hike strenuous.

ROUND TRIP HIKING DISTANCE: About 6 miles.

APPROXIMATE HIKING TIME: 4 hours or more, stops included.

ALTITUDE RANGE: Highest point, 6,547 feet; lowest point, 5,450 feet; total vertical ascent, 1,100 feet.

SEASONAL CONSIDERATIONS: Too hot in summer. Road may not be passable after heavy rain or snow.

ROUND TRIP DRIVING: 42 miles, about 2 hours.

DRIVING DIRECTIONS: Take Washington Avenue north from the Plaza. Turn left in front of the pink-stuccoed Scottish Rite Temple onto Paseo de Peralta. At the intersection with Guadalupe Street, turn right and follow Guadalupe which joins Highway 84/285. Continue north on Highway 84/285 to Camino de la Tierra on your left just past the median wall. This is about 2.5 miles from the plaza. Turn left onto Camino de la Tierra. Take your mileage at the turnoff. You will be driving on this road (which becomes Buckman Road after a while) all the way down to the Rio Grande. The first 5.5 miles are paved and take you to the La Tierra development. Occasionally, the road splits, and there will be trees and bushes separating the two lanes. Stay on the right lane and go straight ahead at intersections. On the unpaved section of the road, you will encounter washboard surface, cattle guards, and ruts or deep sand where the road is crossed by drainages. Slow down!

About 11 miles from the turnoff onto La Tierra Road you will pass a windmill and a corral on your left. Your road now parallels Cañada Ancha (a sandy arroyo) and the basalt-capped edge of the Caja del Rio vol-

canic field on the left. Soon, the vertical
walls of Diablo Canyon (called Caja del Rio
Canyon on the topo map) will appear ahead of
you to the left. At 15.5 miles, you will
pass the turnoff (on the left) to Diablo
Canyon. Further down the road, ignore two
roads that go off to the right. Drive
slowly and look for ruts. The last few road
miles can be bad! A grove of tamarisks
ahead will tell you that the river is near.
Shortly after the Rio Grande comes in sight,
the road turns left and up to an open spot.
Park your car here. You have driven 18 1/2
miles from the La Tierra turnoff.

HIKING INSTRUCTIONS: Before starting the
hike, you may want to spend a few minutes at
the bank of the river. Its muddy waters are
always a welcome sight in this dry country.
Upstream, to your right, Buckman Mesa rises
steeply. No trail going up is to be seen
from here. This hike will take you to the
east side of the mesa before you start the
ascent. First, go back on the road that you
just drove on. While still in the tamarisk
grove, look for a secondary road that goes
off to the left. Follow this road for some
five minutes to a fence (with a gate) and
some 30 yards beyond the fence to a wide
arroyo that comes in from the right. Check
the time here, turn right and follow the
arroyo upstream, in an easterly direction.
Soon, the arroyo narrows into a canyon with
vertical walls cut through compacted sand.
Keep an eye on the left wall of the canyon.
After 10 to 15 minutes of hiking in the
arroyo, you will see a rough trail on the
left climbing out of the canyon toward Buckman Mesa. The trail is usually marked by
cairns. You will be coming back on this
trail.

For now, stay in the canyon. Some 30 yards
after passing the trail, you will see a
small arroyo coming in from the left at
ground level, creating a break in the canyon
wall and affording you a glimpse of the
southern tip of Buckman Mesa. Continue in
the main canyon. Soon, it widens, and Buckman Mesa will appear on your left again.
You can clearly discern the dark, basaltic
top that protects the underlying layers of
ash and sand from erosion. Below the banded
ash strata, sand and talus form a more
gentle slope. As you follow the arroyo,
make sure you are in the main drainage (the
one that follows the base of Buckman Mesa).
Ignore branches that fork to the right.
After hiking some 45 minutes (a little under
2 miles), you will come to a dirt road that
cuts across your arroyo. There may be a
sign "GAS PIPELINE." Turn left onto this
road. It runs parallel to Buckman Mesa (in
a northeasterly direction) and goes slightly
uphill.

Ahead of you, on the slope of Buckman Mesa,
you may notice an old road zigzagging down.
This will be your route of ascent. For now,
follow the road you are on for about five
minutes, as long as it goes uphill. When
you come to a saddle (road starts to descend
ahead of you), stop. Scrutinize the mesa
slope on your left. You may be able to de-
tect the badly eroded old cart road that
comes down from the top. It looks more like
a gully. Gullies don't zigzag, however.
You can't see if or where the road reaches
the bottom. Start going up toward the mesa
top, staying on the ridge that comes down to
the saddle. In a few minutes you will come
to the "gully" (the eroded road) where it
makes a turn. Follow the "gully" up. Soon,
it turns into a rough, rocky road. After 15
to 20 minutes of climbing, the road crosses

layers of compacted ash and comes to a fence. After going through a gap in the fence, it continues in the same direction for about 15 yards, then it turns right and zigzags up over basalt rocks to the top of the mesa. Otowi Peak, less than a mile away, is not visible yet.

If you recognize the road (it shows as a cut or indentation in the rocks) follow it for some 5 minutes until it peters out. Continue in the same direction for another minute or so, and Otowi Peak will appear ahead of you. Eureka! If you lose the road early on, go in a westerly direction (about 90° west of MAGNETIC north) until you can see Otowi Peak. Head for the peak across the flat mesa top and past an old corral. You should be at the foot of the peak some 20 minutes after seeing it for the first time. Going up, take the path of least resistance and avoid steep, rocky parts if possible. If, some 30 to 40 yards below the top, you come upon a faint, fairly level trail, you might want to follow it to the left (west). It leads to the "blowhole," an opening into the underworld, dating back to the days when the volcano was spewing steam or hot gases. Danger! Do not attempt to explore this hole. It is deep enough to get you into trouble. On the way to the blowhole, and right on top of Otowi Peak, you may come across some petroglyphs. Above all, enjoy the views from the top. White Rock Canyon and the Jemez Mountains are to the west, Otowi Bridge appears to the north, Black Mesa to the northeast. Far to the northeast and east, you will see the Sangre de Cristo Mountains, and closer by, to the south, the Caja del Rio volcanic field.

Special note: Otowi Peak is just south of the San Ildefonso Indian reservation boundary line, beyond which a permit is needed, so respect the land and do not wander any farther north than the peak itself.

Before leaving the peak, take time to study your topo map and look at the terrain to the south. (Interesting fact: the rocks on the peak are magnetic and compass readings will be inaccurate.) To the south, Buckman Mesa ends in two "fingers." For the most part, the mesa edge ends in vertical cliffs. However, BETWEEN the fingers, where a drainage goes down, the terrain is less steep. That is where your trail descends. From Otowi Peak to the descending trail there is no path. From the peak, the two fingers are clearly visible. The finger on the right (west) is higher than the finger on the left. It will be clearly visible most of the time when you go toward the trail. Use it to orient yourself.

Leave Otowi Peak, going down the easiest way in a southeasterly direction. After 10 minutes or so, you will be on fairly level ground. Your trail off the mesa top is less than a mile (about 20 minutes) away. Start going in a southerly direction and keep an eye on the right "finger" that appears ahead of you to the right. If you come too close to the western edge of the mesa, you will have to cross steep gullies. In about 20 minutes, you should come to a drainage that goes in a southerly direction. Before it starts to go down steeply, there should be a faint trail marked by little cairns. This is your trail between the two fingers.

Before heading down, you may want to make a little side trip to an overlook. You are at the place where the two fingers come together. Follow the left (eastern) finger to its end (it takes about 5 minutes). You

will have great views to the south and down
into the canyon where you started the hike.
Go back to the trail that will take you
down.

If you did not find the trail or the drainage in the first place, keep on going south
until you reach the edge of the mesa and the
tip of one of the two fingers. With the
help of the topo map, you will be able to
figure out where you are. The eastern
finger goes farthest to the south and is
narrow and grassy (no trees) toward the
end. The western finger is higher and
wider. Go back to where the fingers meet
and look for the trail. It is marked by
little cairns.

The descent will take 30 minutes or longer.
The trail soon goes to the right (west) side
of the drainage and stays there all the way
down. Where the trail is eroded, look for a
cairn to guide you. Footing is poor and
rocks are loose, so be careful. When you
come to the canyon at the bottom of the
mesa, turn right and retrace your steps back
to the car.

Note: You can reach Otowi Peak by a shorter
way (about 4 miles round trip). Start the
hike as described in the instructions. Go
up the arroyo. After 15 minutes or so, you
come to the place where the trail climbs out
of the arroyo (to your left). This is the
return trail described above. Follow the
trail up to the edge of the mesa top. Memorize this place before you continue toward
Otowi Peak, which is a little under a mile
to the north of you. Climb Otowi Peak and
return the same way you came as described in
the hiking instructions.

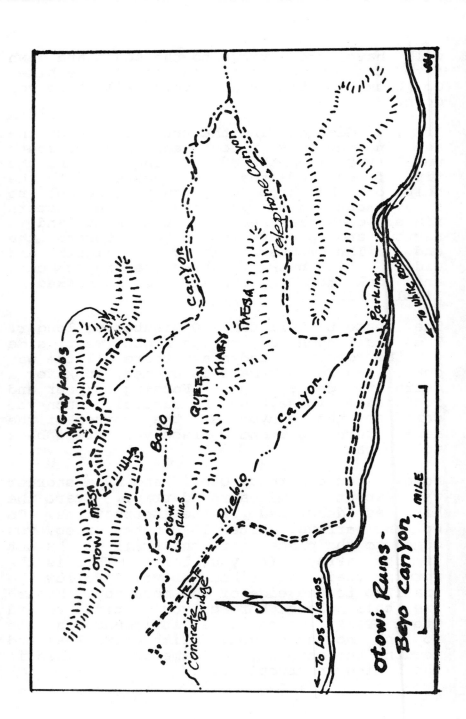

Otowi Ruins – Bayo Canyon

1 MILE

OTOWI RUINS - BAYO CANYON

by
Arnold and Carolyn Keskulla

U.S. GEOLOGICAL SURVEY MAPS REQUIRED: Puye and at the very beginning White Rock - 7.5 minute series.

SALIENT FEATURES: Ancient ruins, cave dwellings, lovely views of Sangre de Cristo, Jemez and Taos Mountains from mesa tops, pleasant walking in canyon bottoms, beautiful seasonal flowers. Most of this hike is off trail. It should not be attempted unless a member of the group is experienced in reading topo maps and is able to locate the position of the hikers on the map.

RATING: Moderate/strenuous.

ROUND TRIP HIKING DISTANCE: Seven to eight miles.

APPROXIMATE HIKING TIME: Four to five hours, with stops.

ALTITUDE RANGE: Highest point, 6600 feet; lowest point, 6000 feet; total vertical ascent, 700 feet.

SEASONAL CONSIDERATIONS: Spring, fall, winter if not too much snow. Probably too hot in midsummer.

ROUND TRIP DRIVING: 57 miles - 1 1/4 hours.

DRIVING DIRECTIONS: Take Highway 285 north to Pojoaque. Just beyond Pueblo Plaza, about 16 miles north of Santa Fe, turn left (west) on State Road 502 toward Los Alamos. The road crosses the Rio Grande and climbs to a well-marked 'Y' intersection about 28 miles from Santa Fe. The right leg of the 'Y,' which you do not take, goes to Bandelier National Monument and White Rock. Go straight ahead (left leg of the 'Y') toward Los Alamos for 0.3 mile. Turn right into a paved road leading off toward a maintenance yard. Park before the gate, making sure to leave room for large trucks to get by you. The hikers' gate is just ahead (northwest).

HIKING INSTRUCTIONS: Go through the hikers' gate and follow the left hand gravel road northwesterly through ponderosa pines with a view of Tschicoma Peak ahead. After 1.5 miles cross a small bridge over the outlet from the Los Alamos sewer plant. Turn right (north) almost immediately on an old road up a slight incline near a large white half-buried rock. The road curves east and north and is badly eroded in places. After about 1/2 mile there will be a walkers' gate through a fence surrounding the overgrown ruins of Otowi Pueblo.

After viewing the ruins, backtrack about 100 feet and go down into Bayo Canyon (to the north). Go east on the sandy bottom about 1/8 mile or more, then look for a suitable place to go up the mesa apron on a long diagonal (northeast) to the base of the orange cliffs. (You will not be following a trail here, so watch for loose rocks.) As you come up against the cliff face of Otowi Mesa, turn right. You will find many ancient caves with soot-blackened ceilings, viga holes, Moki stairways and old accumulations of dung from burros or sheep. In front of this cliff there are also some lovely flowers in the late summer, such as Rocky Mountain bee plant, and an unusual white gilia with blue anthers. Continue around the end of the cliff and a few hundred yards more (northwest) until you find the only manageable way to get up to the mesa top (mark it in case you should decide to return this way rather than completing the hike).

Go as far up the mesa as you care to, enjoying the lovely views of the mountains in all directions. You will see to the northwest that this mesa joins another mesa which has two large gray domes. Go down a little to the other mesa and then proceed eastward past one gray dome to just before the other. In this area find the only manageable way down off this mesa (about 1 mile from getting on top of it). At the time of this writing there were two small cairns close to the edge of the cliff marking the top of this descent.

Angle steeply downward (southeast) over the loose rocks to a small sandy-bottomed canyon that soon joins Bayo Canyon. From this junction continue down Bayo Canyon (east) for about 1.5 miles (approximately 45 minutes) to the first major arroyo on the right. There were at the time of this writing two small cairns marking this side canyon. Looking up this canyon you will see the 'Queen Mary' mesa (which has been on your right) end-on. Go up this winding side canyon (west south west) until almost the end. You will get glimpses of a telephone line occasionally and once it will cross over the canyon. Finally, take a path on the left up under the pole line to the ridge at the top of the canyon - about 1.5 miles from the junction. Now make a sharp left turn and go down through the woods toward the Los Alamos road (visible and audible) and the maintenance yard (sometimes visible).   Skirt this to your left to your car (about 1/2 mile from the ridge top).

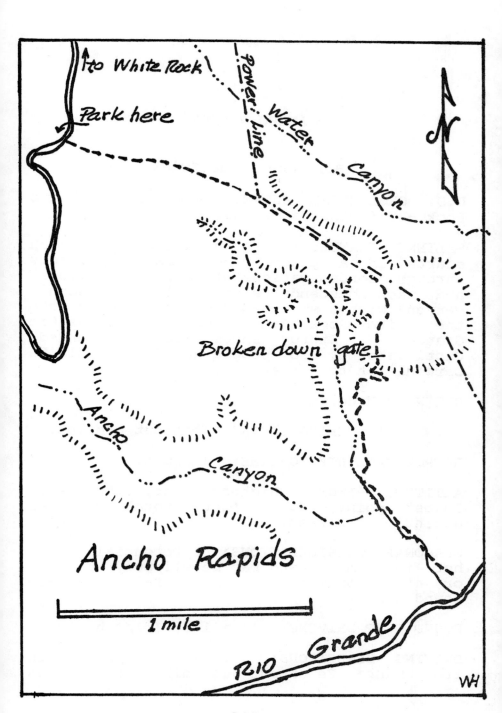

ANCHO RAPIDS

by
Bill and Linda Zwick

U.S. GEOLOGICAL SURVEY MAP REQUIRED: White
Rock - 7.5 minutes series.

SALIENT FEATURES: A pleasant walk which
starts in a piñon pine forest, proceeds
through concentrations of juniper and yucca,
and then descends steeply into a scenic
canyon with a spring-fed stream feeding into
the White Rock Canyon section of the Rio
Grande. Sturdy shoes are recommended.
Cacti abound, so people and dogs should be
careful not to get spines in their feet.

RATING: Moderate.

ROUND TRIP HIKING DISTANCE: About 6 miles.

APPROXIMATE HIKING TIME: 3 hours.

ALTITUDE RANGE: Highest point, 6,500 feet;
lowest point, 5,460 feet; total vertical
ascent, 1,040 feet.

SEASONAL CONSIDERATIONS: Potentially very
hot in summer and may be slippery when wet
or after snowfall, but generally a year-
round hike.

ROUND TRIP DRIVING: 80 miles; 1 1/2 hours.

DRIVING DIRECTIONS: Take US 84/285 north
from Santa Fe about 16 miles to the Los

Alamos and Bandelier exit (west, left) which is State Road 502. Travel west on State Road 502 for 11 1/2 miles and take the exit toward Bandelier National Monument and the town of White Rock (heading south). After 5 more miles, you arrive at White Rock's only traffic signal (the intersection with Pajarito Road). Carefully check your odometer reading here and drive on straight through the traffic signal, still heading south. Continue on toward Bandelier National Monument for about 3.4 miles to a gate on the left side of the road which is difficult to see from the road. You might find it necessary to pull off on the right shoulder of the road (but the road is narrow here) to see the gate and the small graveled parking area. Traffic in this area moves rapidly around blind curves, so take appropriate care in pulling into the parking area. (Note: If you have taken a hair-pin curve to the left over an arroyo and then up a moderate hill to find a gate, you've gone too far! If the walking entrance through the fence is a simple opening, you are at the wrong gate and you should go back .2 miles toward White Rock.) The large gate will probably be locked due to a recent DOE crack-down on motor vehicle traffic in the area. Pedestrian access is through a V-shaped gate to the right of the large gate.

HIKING INSTRUCTIONS: Proceed through the V-shaped pedestrian access. The hike to the rim of the canyon follows a road built for the installation of powerlines in the area and is relatively uneventful. However, this portion of the hike toward the Rio Grande provides spectacular vistas of the Sangre de Cristo mountains (especially nice in the fall when the aspen are golden) and the return hike provides nice views of the Jemez mountains and Bandelier. You will cross under a powerline which heads north and south and about a mile into the hike the road will converge with another powerline which heads east. Note the radio telescope dish to your right (south) - this Los Alamos facility is part of an array of radio telescopes stretching from the South Pacific to the continental U.S. Continue walking on the road eastward. Looking down, you might notice large ant hills shimmering in the sunlight - a result of the ants mining quartz grains in making their homes.

About 1 3/4 miles from the start of the hike, the road will descend and then begin to rise toward the canyon rim. Shortly after you begin ascending, a spur will leave the road to the right (southeast). Take this spur to its end (approximately 1/2 mile). At this point you are at the rim of Ancho Canyon. Note the broken-down fence and gate which used to prevent grazing cattle from descending into the canyon. Bear to your right (toward the sandstone cliff) and you will find a trail winding through rockfall which will then begin a relatively steep traverse to the bottom of the canyon. The trail shows little sign of use, is eroded and rocky in places, but is easy to follow.

At the bottom of the canyon, the trail is mostly obvious, but cairns aid your travel here. When the canyon bottom levels out, you will find a spring-fed stream to your right. It's a nice place to rest after your climb down or before beginning your climb back up. The authors shared this rest spot with a large, but shy black bear! The river is not far from here and the trail and cairns will take you to the water's edge.

You can explore the bank of the river varying distances, depending on the water level. Note the dead tamarisk and oak high on the river banks - a result of the high water level of Cochiti Reservoir several years ago. Rocks and debris washed from Ancho Canyon in flash floods have formed Ancho ("wide" in Spanish) Rapid, the most difficult rapid in White Rock Canyon for the river runners who boat past.

To return, retrace your steps. On the way back up the scree slope, notice the huge cholla next to a large old log at the corner of one of the switchbacks. And pick up a large piece of the pumice which is so light; see if a companion has a camera and will take a photograph of you impressively lifting massive rocks with apparent ease.

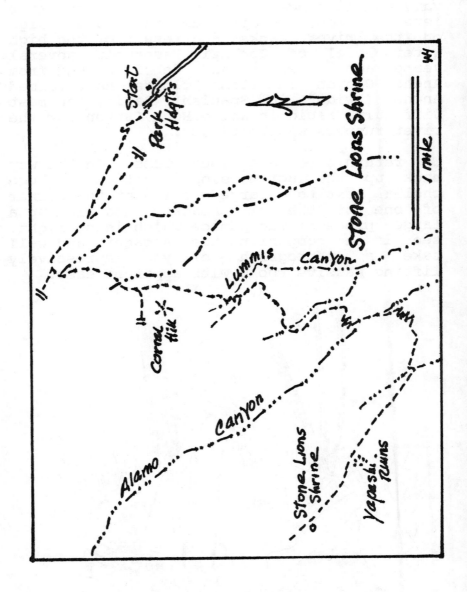

STONE LIONS SHRINE
(BANDELIER NATIONAL MONUMENT)

by
Mickey Bogert

U.S. GEOLOGICAL SURVEY MAP REQUIRED: Frijoles - 7.5 minute series.

SALIENT FEATURES: This is a challenging walk to an ancient shrine showing signs of current use by Indians from the nearby pueblos. Driving to the trailhead is no problem. There are paved roads all the way. It is a strenuous hike because of the climbs in and out of several beautiful canyons, especially Alamo.

The walks across the mesa tops are easy, on good trails, with views of the Sangre de Cristo and Jemez Mountains. Vegetation is mostly piñon-juniper with some ponderosa pine. Just before the Stone Lions Shrine is a large, unexcavated pueblo ruin. Note: It is unlawful to remove anything from the National Monument, especially Indian arti-facts. No dogs are allowed in the National Monument. Carry plenty of water.

RATING: Strenuous.

ROUND TRIP HIKING DISTANCE: 12.8 miles.

APPROXIMATE HIKING TIME: 8 hours.

ALTITUDE RANGE: Highest point, 6660 feet; lowest point, 6066 feet; total vertical ascent, 2700 feet.

SEASONAL CONSIDERATIONS: Can be uncomfortably hot in summer.

ROUND TRIP DRIVING: 92 miles - approximately 2.5 hours.

DRIVING DIRECTIONS: Take U.S. Highway 285 north from Santa Fe to Pojoaque. Just beyond Pueblo Plaza, about 16 miles north of Santa Fe, turn left (west) on State Highway 502. The road crosses the Rio Grande and climbs to a well-marked "Y" intersection about 28 miles from Santa Fe. The left leg of the "Y" (which you do not take) goes to Los Alamos. Take the right leg, State Route 4, toward Bandelier and White Rock. The entrance to Bandelier is beyond White Rock about 12.5 miles from the "Y." There is an entrance fee of $5 per car, except for senior citizens or holders of Golden Eagle Passports. Drive to the Visitor Center and across the bridge over the Rio Frijoles, turn left, and park in the area designated for back country hikers.

HIKING INSTRUCTIONS: From the parking area, walk back up the paved road, past the bridge for a few hundred feet where you will see a sign on your left which will identify the trails to the Stone Lions and Frijolito Ruin. Turn left (southwest) onto this trail. The Stone Lions Trail soon branches from the Frijolito Ruin Trail and heads northwest (right). This is a fairly gradual climb and affords good views of the ruins in Frijoles Canyon. When you reach the top of the mesa you can see Ceremonial Cave, with the long ladders leading up to it, directly across the canyon. The Frijolito Trail rejoins the Stone Lions Trail near this

point, and a few yards farther on is a
junction (1 mile from the Visitor Center).
At this junction, follow the sign pointing
left (south) to the Corral Hill-Stone Lions
Trail.

A little over half a mile beyond this
junction you will pass the Corral Hill Trail
going off to your right. Continue on the
Stone Lions Trail, crossing Lummis Canyon
(identified by a sign) and its two tributary
canyons on each side of it, and then on to
the rim of Alamo Canyon.

For most of this distance the vegetation is
varied: Juniper, piñon pine and some ponderosa, or yellow, pine, as well as yucca and
cactus. The previous canyon crossings are
semishaded and fairly easy, so Alamo Canyon
comes as a shock, as well as a spectacular
surprise. There are beautiful views, but no
shade, and there is a very steep switchback
trail down a precipitous cliff. It is essential to carry sufficient water, for it
requires a great deal of effort to descend
500 feet in 0.3 miles and make a similar
ascent on the other side. And you must do
it again, in reverse, on the way back.

The canyon bottom does have trees, and a
stream during certain times of the year. Do
not drink the water. The trail goes downstream for several hundred yards before
crossing and starting upwards. The rim of
the canyon is a good place for a snack
break, to enjoy the view, and to gather
strength for the next two miles. A half
mile farther on is a shallow canyon, a
tributary of Alamo, about 80 feet deep. The
vegetation south of Alamo is quite different: more arid in appearance, no more
ponderosa, and the junipers and piñons are
shorter. Cactus is much more abundant.

(From here on, when snow covered, the trail may be difficult to follow.)

One mile beyond the little canyon, in a westerly direction, is Yapashi Pueblo, now a mound of rubble. From here you will have magnificent views of many mountains. To the west, the San Miguel Mountains; south, the Sandias; southeast, the Ortiz and San Pedro Mountains; northwest, the Jemez; and to the northeast, the Sangre de Cristo Mountains. A half mile beyond the Yapashi ruins, on your left, you will see a small enclosure made of piled up stones. In the middle of this is what is left of the stone lion carvings. Time and the elements have obliterated the heads but the backs and haunches remain. Sometimes there are offerings of deer antlers hanging on the trees in back of the lions but more often antlers are racked around them, almost like a wreath. Most of us who come here sense a special atmosphere about this place. Remember that it is a sacred area to many people, so please respect and enjoy it accordingly.

Return to your car over the same trails.

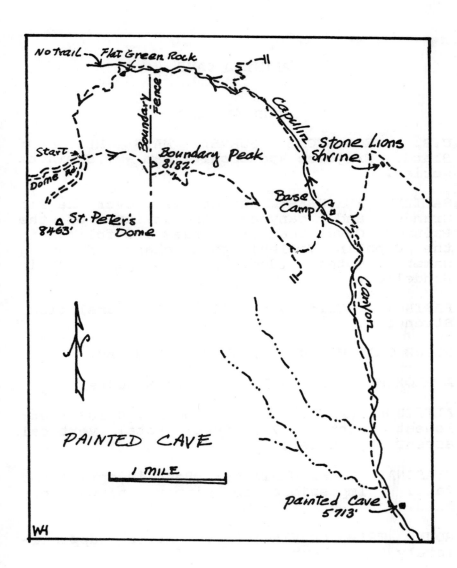

No Trail — Flat Green Rock

Boundary Fence

Capulin

Stone Lions Shrine

Start

Dome №1

Boundary Peak
8182'

△ St. Peter's
8463'   Dome

Base
Camp

Canyon

N

PAINTED CAVE

1 MILE

Painted Cave
5713'

W4

PAINTED CAVE

by
John Masters

U.S. GEOLOGICAL SURVEY MAPS REQUIRED: Bland, Frijoles and Cochiti Dam - 7.5 minute series.

SALIENT FEATURES: Great views over the Rio Grande and canyons; Indian art of the Painted Cave; beautiful trees and foliage in the Capulin Valley; good chance of seeing game. Note: dogs are not permitted in Bandelier.

RATING: Mild sweat. (Editor's translation: Strenuous.)

ROUND TRIP HIKING DISTANCE: 15 miles.

APPROXIMATE HIKING TIME: 7 to 8 hours.

ALTITUDE RANGE: Highest point, 8,108 feet; lowest point, 5,713 feet; total vertical ascent, 2,400 feet.

SEASONAL CONSIDERATIONS: Best in spring and fall. Impossible in winter unless very mild.

ROUND TRIP DRIVING: 97 miles - approximately 3 1/4 hours.

DRIVING DIRECTIONS: Take Highway 84/285 north out of Santa Fe to Pojoaque. Just beyond Pueblo Plaza, about 16 miles from

Santa Fe, turn left (west) onto State Road 502. The road crosses the Rio Grande and climbs to a well marked "Y" intersection about 28 miles from Santa Fe. The left leg of the "Y" (which you do not take) goes to Los Alamos. Take the right leg (State Route 4) toward Bandelier and White Rock. After about 1.5 miles from the "Y," turn right. After another 5.7 miles you will come to a "Y." Do not take the right lane, but take the left curve. Continue past a series of lights, onto Loop #4. In another 5.4 miles you will come to a "T" intersection with Route 4. This intersection is called the West Gate of Los Alamos. Turn right here. The road winds and twists and the scenery is beautiful. After about 6 miles from the West Gate you will come to Forest Road #289.

Turn left here and go straight past a sign reading "Leaving Bandelier" and over a cattle guard at 2.1 miles from where you turned onto #289. The cattle guard marks the Forest Service boundary. Note your odometer reading at this cattle guard. You have 8.6 miles more to go to reach the trailhead.

Stay on #289 until you come to another "T" junction. Take the left turn onto Forest Road #142. This junction will be about 5 miles from the cattle guard. Stay on FS 142 for 3.5 miles, passing several secondary roads to the left and right which you do not take, and you will be at the trailhead. Park as the road turns sharp right and comes out on a steep edge overlooking the Rio Grande canyons. This is St. Peter's Dome Lookout Corner and the trailhead. Park to the left where there are signs indicating the trailhead. You will start down Boundary Peak Trail #427 and return on Capulin Canyon Trail #116.

HIKING INSTRUCTIONS: This is a very beautiful walk, especially in fall, from the
colors; and in spring, from the rush of
water in the Capulin. Look for great cliff
formations of tuff as you drop into Capulin
Canyon; distant views of Tschicoma and
Caballo Mountains, and the Truchas Peaks
across the whole valley; all three types of
juniper - common, Rocky Mountain and alligator; magnificent stands of ponderosa pine;
hoof/paw marks and scats of black bear,
deer, elk and wild burro (all these seem to
use the area freely); tremendous views over
Jemez canyons; fingerling trout in the
Capulin; and, always, the half hidden things
- the wildflowers, small animals, the birds.

The walk is all down, then all up. If it's
too hot, have a dip in the stream before
starting the final ascent.

From the parking area, take Trail 427
heading, at that point, northeast (signposted); it turns east and wends down the
side of Boundary Peak. At about one hour
(altitude 6660 feet) you come to a junction
signposted to Turkey Springs and Dome Lookout. Ignore the instructions, put your back
to the sign and follow your trail north,
down into Capulin Canyon (great views opposite). After about 15 minutes (6,200 feet),
cross the Rio Capulin at a large log building called, and signposted, "Base Camp."
More signs here to be ignored as you continue right (southeast) downstream. In 5
minutes you pass an Adirondack shelter on
the left. From behind this, a trail (signposted) leads to the Stone Lions. Proceed
on downstream, with several stream crossings
(which are great fun in spring), for about
another 45 minutes (5713 feet), where you
will see the big scooped out overhang of the
Painted Cave to your left (northeast). A

trail (signposted) takes off to it, crossing the stream. Do not attempt to climb up to the cave itself. It's dangerous and it's not allowed, to protect the art and the cave.

When you're ready to return, go back the same way you came, as far as Base Camp. Do NOT cross the stream here, but continue north upstream past a sign reading "Trail." After about 45 minutes you come to a trail fork (6600 feet) where a trail goes off right. You follow the sign "Dome Lookout 3" and keep on roughly west, up river. Thirty minutes later you reach the fence which shows that you are leaving Bandelier National Monument. About 15 minutes after that, at the first crossing of the Capulin after the boundary fence, cross to the true right bank (i.e., right when facing downstream) and look for the trail up the hill. There is a grey green flat rock 7 by 12 feet in the clearing here. Go on 20 paces past it due south toward the slope. The trail takes off right (west-southwest) in the trees along the foot of the slope. It's difficult to miss this as there is no trail on up the river, after a hundred feet or so. Climb steadily, well graded path, more great views, mostly behind you, to the cars; and you will find that you have come up on Capulin Canyon Trail #116.

Obviously this walk can be done in the reverse direction.

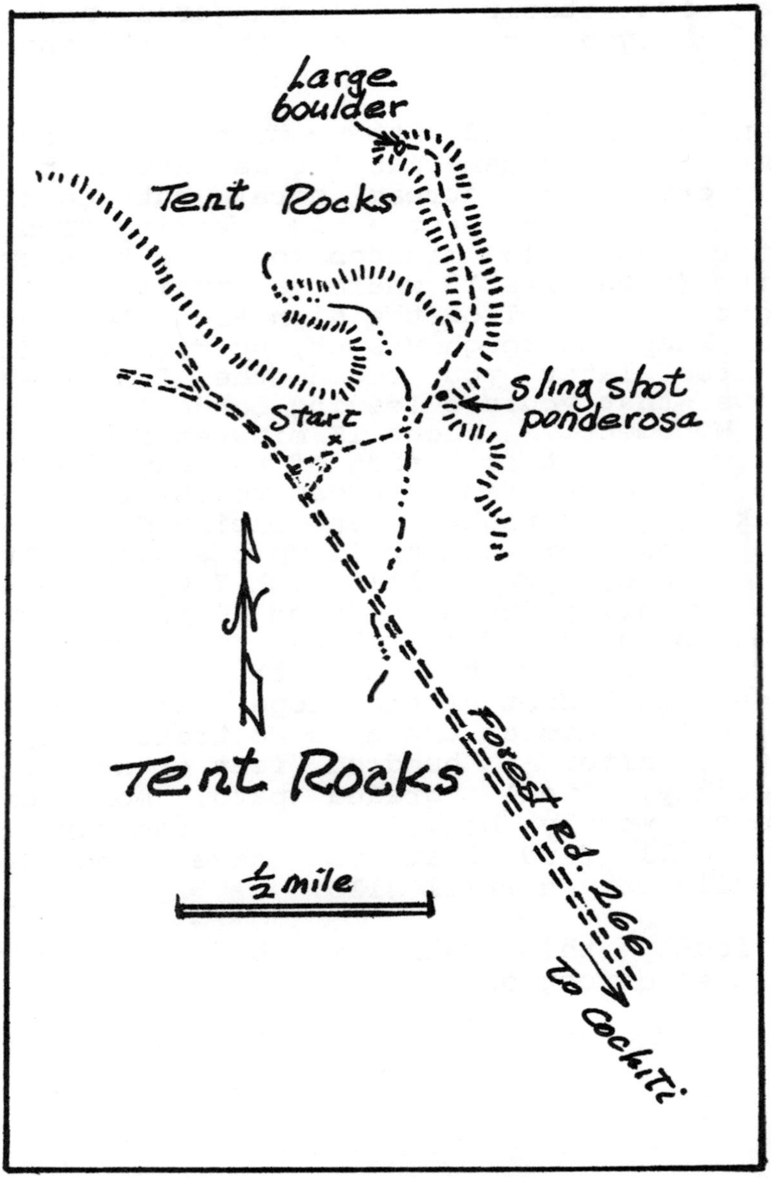

Large boulder

Tent Rocks

sling shot ponderosa

Start

N

Tent Rocks

½ mile

Forest Rd. 266

To Cochiti

TENT ROCKS

by
Alan and Jenny Karp

U.S. GEOLOGICAL SURVEY MAP REQUIRED: Cañada - 7.5 minute series.

SALIENT FEATURES: Fascinating miniature canyon with unbelievable tuff rock formations. There are wildflowers in season. Spring or fall or early summer morning hours make this an idyllic short comfortable hike. The canyon is very photogenic but whether you bring a camera or not, the banded striations, shadowed cliffs, and gravity defiant rocks will be ever with you. You will probably want to explore the tent rocks near the road after you return to your car.

RATING: Easy.

ROUND TRIP HIKING DISTANCE: 3 miles.

APPROXIMATE HIKING TIME: 1.5 hours.

ALTITUDE RANGE: Highest point, 6,100 feet; lowest point, 5,900 feet; total vertical ascent, 200 feet.

SEASONAL CONSIDERATIONS: Not a winter hike if there has been heavy snowfall.

ROUND TRIP DRIVING: 80 miles - approximately 2 hours.

DRIVING DIRECTIONS: Take I-25 south toward Albuquerque and get off at the Cochiti exit

264.   Take the right turn (west) off the exit ramp onto State Road 16. In about 8 miles you will come to a "T" intersection. Turn right here onto State Road 22 and follow this road for about 2 1/2 miles. Look for an intersection where you will take a sharp turn left (still State Road #22) toward Cochiti Pueblo.   Stay on this road for 1.7 miles. To the right of the road you will see a water tower painted like an Indian drum and then a similar, but narrower tower.   At the second tower turn right onto a gravel road. This is Forest Road #266. A sign at the intersection is marked "Bear Springs."   In about 3 miles you will pass over a cattle guard and in a little less than 1.5 miles after the cattle guard, you will see a well-used, triangular driveway to the right. You will now be in sight of some of the tent rock formations. Turn right and park.

HIKING INSTRUCTIONS: Start walking here along the side road which has stones blocking vehicular entrance and a sign declaring it closed to vehicular use. Bear right when in doubt, at one point taking what looks more like a narrow wash than a road.   About 7 minutes into the hike you will reach a larger wash or arroyo. As you approach it you will see straight ahead what appears to be two ponderosa trees close together.   On closer approach this will turn out to be a distinctive double-header "sling-shot" ponderosa on the right side of the arroyo.   This tree is a key reference point which assures you you are in the correct arroyo.   Continue up the arroyo which branches and then comes together again and which leads you into an enchanting narrow canyon.

Mother Nature's imagination went wild in this stone wonderland. Over the ages, wind

and water have sensuously carved out this
inspiring miniature canyon, only 40 miles
from Santa Fe. This micro Grand Canyon
envelopes and entices you with its cap rocks
and volcanic tuff, ponderosa-lined trail and
cheerful wildflowers. It gives you a very
special spiritual feeling.

The arroyo funnels into this enticing inner
sanctuary. As you wind your way up the canyon, the soft curving walls provide you with
meditative niches. The sky appears a deeper
blue than imaginable and provides a dramatic
backdrop for the still-forming tent rocks.

Approximately fifteen minutes into the hike,
a tall ponderosa and a lone tent rock appear
at the base of the left wall of the canyon.
The wall bears petroglyphs depicting a serpent, handprints and other symbols.

The miniature canyon narrows into a stone
hallway in which at several places you must
scramble over rock steps. At one point you
will need to crawl on hands and knees under
a huge boulder. Some hikers may require a
helping hand or a boost. The trail continues to wind, alternating between open and
more narrow sections. You will finally
arrive at a boulder in a fall of small rocks
going up through a narrow passage. Access
is difficult here and most hikers will make
this the turn-around point of the hike.

For the hardy and more adventurous, a helping hand will be needed to scale the fallen
boulder. If you scale it you will see a
tall ponderosa stump on the left of the
canyon. A trail starts here to your left
paralleling the fallen ponderosa trunk. The
trail ascends a razor-back ridge to the
upper mesa several hundred yards away and

over 400 feet above. The ascent is difficult on a steep trail with poor footing made
slippery by loose gravel and sand. It may
be scary for some. The vista from the mesa
top will give a super northern New Mexico
view; to the east is the familiar shape of
Tetilla Peak above Cochiti Lake, to the
north are the Sangre de Cristo Mountains,
and to the south is an interesting view of
Sandia Peak.

On your return, after leaving the canyon,
watch for the sling-shot ponderosa pine so
you will know when to leave the main arroyo
and find your way back to your car.

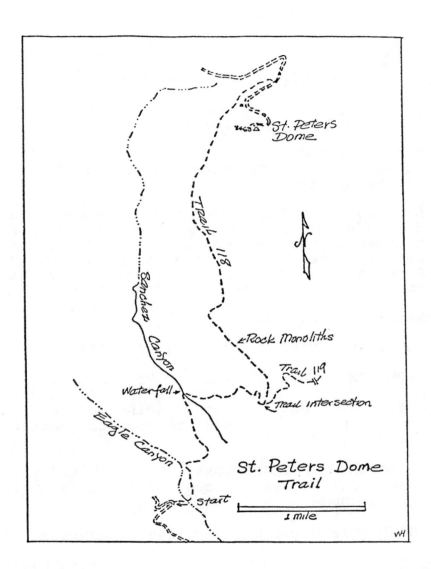

St. Peters
Dome

Trail 118

Sanchez Canyon

Rock Monoliths

Trail 119

Waterfall

Trail intersection

Eagle Canyon

start

St. Peters Dome
Trail

1 mile

N

VH

ST. PETER'S DOME TRAIL

by
Kristin Eppler

U.S. GEOLOGICAL SURVEY MAPS REQUIRED: Cañada, Bland, Frijoles and Cochiti Dam, 7.5 minute series.

SALIENT FEATURES: Best western access trail to Dome Wilderness and Bandelier National Monument. Unusual volcanic rock formations, active waterfall, extensive views of the Sandias, Ortiz, San Pedros, Caja Del Rio, Cochiti Dam, and Sangre de Cristos.

RATING: Strenuous.

ROUND TRIP HIKING DISTANCE: 12 miles.

APPROXIMATE HIKING TIME: 7 to 8 hours.

ALTITUDE RANGE: Highest point, 8,464 feet; lowest point - 6,570 feet; total vertical ascent 2,500 feet.

SEASONAL CONSIDERATIONS: Can be hiked year-round when access is open; high temperatures during summer.

ROUND TRIP DRIVING: 80 miles; 2 hours.

DRIVING DIRECTIONS: Take I-25 south toward Albuquerque. At Exit #264 turn right onto Highway 16 to a T junction with Highway 22. Turn right on 22 to Cochiti Village, which is beyond the Dam. Take your mileage at the Village. Continue for 2.7 miles past the

Cochiti golf course to Forest Road #289. If there is no sign at this corner you can identify the intersection by the Cochiti Stables on your left. Turn right on Forest Road 289. You will cross a cattle guard with a Forest Service warning that the road is unsuitable for passenger cars. This road is passable when dry. When wet or snow-covered, the road is unsuitable and treacherous for any vehicle. Forest Road 289 is often closed during winter months. At 3.8 miles, the road crosses a shallow ford (Rio Chiquito). You may wish to check the depth during spring runoff. At 4.8 miles, you cross the Forest Boundary. At 6.2 miles, you will approach a climbing left turn and at this point on your right you will see a Forest Service sign marking the trail head (Forest Trail #118). Park your car at this corner.

HIKING INSTRUCTIONS: The Forest Service sign indicates the direction of Forest Trail 118 and your destination, St. Peter's Dome, 6 miles. Another sign may be here indicating that a permit is required. This permit applies only to overnight camping, so for this hike it can be ignored.

In the fall of 1989 the routing of the beginning of this trail (about 1 1/2 miles) was changed in order to avoid a very difficult crossing of the head of Eagle Canyon. At this time, the new trail was marked by red ribbons tied onto trees and bushes. Take this trail, which soon descends steeply into Eagle Canyon and then rises on the opposite side, winding between and around large boulders. After emerging on the other side and following the path and flags over a fairly level area, the new trail joins the old trail over a small gully. Note this junction so you won't miss it on the return trip.

The trail continues in an easy climb and soon overlooks Sanchez Canyon. This area is noted for its massive volcanic outcroppings and is the home of many Alligator Junipers which are easy to identify by their scaly bark. Your trail now swings to your left and descends into Sanchez Canyon on a long gradual traverse to the Rito Sanchez and the Sanchez Falls. The trail crosses the stream just above the falls, turns sharply right and begins to climb. The best location to view the falls is about 100 yards past the stream crossing. An alligator juniper on your left marks an open space for viewing. There is (nonpotable) water in the Rito Sanchez almost every month of the year, and the falls are quite spectacular at times of heavy runoff.

Continue on the trail, which crosses a series of small arroyos. After a number of rocky switchbacks, the trail climbs out of Sanchez Canyon and swings to the left. About one mile after the stream crossing, you will come to an intersection. The trail that continues straight ahead goes to destinations inside Bandelier Monument, as indicated by a sign. Your trail, marked only by a cairn, goes off to the left and uphill. Turn left at this intersection and continue climbing on a well-defined trail that traverses around to a point overlooking Picacho Canyon. The trail now roller-coasters along a gradual climb as it enters Picacho Canyon and soon you pass under a large rock outcropping that produces a small waterfall during spring runoff. During wet years this dripping spring falls on the trail and has been utilized as a welcome shower by overheated hikers.

Your trail now climbs through a conifer forest and continues under many interesting rock monoliths. At the base of Cerro Picacho the trail swings right and traverses along Cerro Picacho's eastern slope, coming out on a steep, rising ridge between Cerro Picacho and St. Peter's Dome. At the base of St. Peter's Dome your trail swings left and traverses the west slope of St. Peter's until it tops out in an abandoned picnic area and connects with St. Peter's Dome Forest Road 142. A half-mile climb up this road brings you to the top of St. Peter's Dome. There are views in every direction. You have now hiked approximately 6 miles and this is an excellent place for lunch (not a safe place during electrical storms, however). Return to your car the same way you hiked up.

This out and back hike on #118 affords many extensive views and has very little use except during deer and elk season. Wear red clothing and leave the dogs at home when the hunters are out.

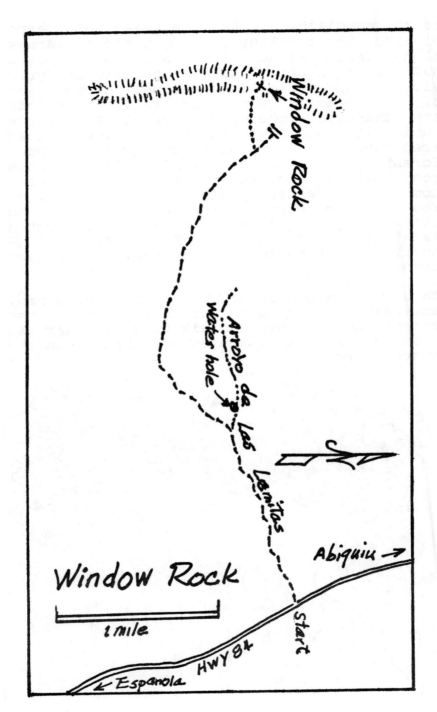

Window Rock

Window Rock

Arroyo de Las Lomitas

Water hole

Abiquiu →

1 mile

Start

HWY 84

← Espanola

WINDOW ROCK

by
Norbert Sperlich

U.S. GEOLOGICAL SURVEY MAPS REQUIRED: Chili
and Medanales - 7.5 minute series. Most of
the hike follows an unmarked, abandoned jeep
trail. To find the trail on the topo maps
(1953 edition), start with the Medanales
map. Look for Highway 84 at the lower mar-
gin of the map. Follow the highway up for
3/4 inch to where Arroyo de las Lemitas
comes in from the left (west). This is the
start of the hike. Follow the arroyo for
1/2 inch and you will see a "T" junction of
jeep trails (indicated by broken lines).
Follow the trail that goes up the arroyo and
into the Chili topo map. There, the trail
leaves the arroyo. It goes back into the
Medanales map, where it comes close to
Window Rock.

SALIENT FEATURES: Since the jeep trail you
are hiking on is not marked or maintained,
this is a hike for experienced hikers only.
Much of the terrain is sandy (look for animal tracks!), but there are some rough and
rocky spots, as well. You will hike in a
sandy arroyo, go up on a ridge through badlands, and come to a "window" or hole that
has been weathered out of a dike (a rock
wall formed by igneous rocks). Great views
from Window Rock and along the way. You are
in the piñon-juniper belt, and you will also
encounter cottonwoods, tamarisk, mountain
mahogany, and a stand of ponderosa pines.

RATING: Moderate.

ROUND TRIP HIKING DISTANCE: About 8 miles.

APPROXIMATE HIKING TIME: 5 hours.

ALTITUDE RANGE: Highest point, 6,463 feet; lowest point, 5,800 feet; total vertical ascent, about 1,000 feet.

SEASONAL CONSIDERATIONS: All seasons, but not recommended in hot weather. If you go in summer, take extra water.

ROUND TRIP DRIVING: 70 miles; 1 1/2 hours or more.

DRIVING DIRECTIONS: Take US 84/285 northbound from Santa Fe to Española. At the first signal light in Española, turn left and cross the Rio Grande. At the next light, turn right. Get in the left lane as you approach the third light and turn left. You are still on US 84/285. About 6 miles north of Española, Route 285 separates from Route 84. Keep on going straight on Route 84. Look for the green mile posts on the right side of the road. Take your mileage at mile 199 (mile post 200 was missing in October 1989). Go 1.1 mile past mile post 199 and look for a grey, barn-like building (made from corrugated sheet metal) on your right. Some 40 yards past this building, a power line crosses the highway, and a paved private driveway goes off to the right. Go just past this driveway and park your car on the side of the highway.

HIKING INSTRUCTIONS: Cross the highway. On the west side of the highway is a fence marked "Property Boundary, National Forest." Cross the fence and go down into a sandy arroyo which comes in from the west. Follow the car tracks that run parallel to the arroyo along its right (north) side. If the tracks are gone, follow the arroyo, staying on its right side. Disregard a jeep trail that goes off to the right. Some 7 minutes or so into the hike, you should see a freestanding, orange-brown rock ahead of you on the right side of the arroyo. In another 5 minutes or so you will be close to this rock. In front of the rock is a rectangular, green water tank and a well. The car tracks (your "trail") pass the tank on the left and go in and out of the arroyo. There are cottonwoods, elm trees, and tamarisks along your way, and sandy hills with piñon and juniper along the sides of the arroyo. Here and there, you will encounter light grey rocks, formed by sand particles that have been cemented together. Often, the surface of these rocks is covered with balls or nodules consisting of cemented sand. These balls come in different sizes: peppercorns, peas, tennis balls, and larger.

A little over a mile into the hike (it seems longer because of the sandy terrain) the arroyo starts to narrow down. Just where it makes a turn to the right, look for a jeep trail that goes out of the arroyo and uphill on your left. This is your trail to Window Rock.

(Note: If you have 20 minutes extra time, though, you might want to continue in the arroyo for a little side trip. Remember the place where the jeep trail climbs out of the arroyo. After passing this spot, follow the arroyo, which turns to the right. On your right, the arroyo is bordered by walls of compacted sand. Scratched into the sand are inscriptions such as LA LOCA PARTY, MARIJUANA, LU ANN. In a few minutes, you will come to a water hole. Beyond the water hole, the terrain becomes rocky and steep.

The water hole is a great place for a stop.
Many birds come here to drink, and you will
hear their songs in the nearby trees. Go
back to where the jeep trail leaves the
arroyo, now on your right.)

The trail climbs to the top of a ridge and
follows the ridge line. Here and there, the
trail is blocked by mounds of dirt. You are
surrounded by badlands dotted with juniper
bushes and mountain mahogany. There are
more of the grey sandstone formations sculpt-
ed by the elements. About 20 minutes after
leaving the arroyo, you come to a high point
on the ridge, with splendid views in all
directions. Ahead of you are the Jemez Mountains, to the east you will see the Sangre
de Cristo Range, with the flat-topped Black
Mesa in the foreground. As you continue
your hike, the ridge widens and levels out.
Soon, it narrows again and the trail goes
steeply uphill. Here, the ground is covered
with loose rocks, and the going is rough
until you reach level ground again. Ahead
of you, to the left, you will see a ridge
that is crested by a dark rock wall,
sticking out like a spine. Look for a hole
in the rocks. That's Window Rock! For
about 3/4 mile, the jeep trail goes gently
downhill, taking you to a flat, treeless
area. This is a reservoir where water
collects after heavy rains. Window Rock is
to your left. Here you leave the jeep trail
and go toward Window Rock. Just below the
ridge, there is a sandy bank with tall
ponderosa pines. This is a great spot for a
break before ascending the ridge.

Look for a drainage coming down to the left
of Window Rock. Climb up on the rock-strewn
slope to the left of this drainage. As you
near the top of the ridge, bear to the right
and onto a trail leading to the other side

of the dike and to the window. You can take
great pictures looking through the window
toward the east, especially if you have a
wide-angle lens. Caution should be taken if
you climb up on the dike. It is only 6 feet
wide. Do not attempt to cross over the top
of the window. Enjoy the views and the
solitude and return the way you came.

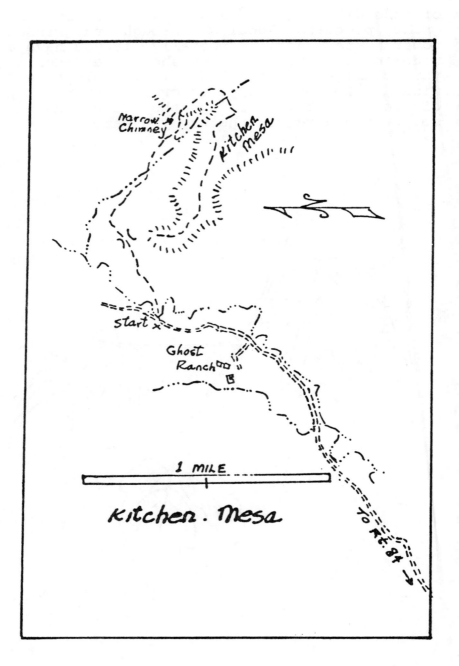

Narrow
Chimney

Kitchen Mesa

start ×

Ghost
Ranch

1 MILE

Kitchen · Mesa

To Rt. 84

KITCHEN MESA

by
Norma McCallan

U.S. GEOLOGICAL SURVEY MAP REQUIRED: Ghost Ranch, 1953, photorevised 1979, 7.5 minute series. Note: this trail does not show on the topo map.

SALIENT FEATURES: All-season access and hiking possibilities; striking vistas, interesting geological features; the best display of red rock in northern New Mexico. The origin of the term Kitchen Mesa is unknown. The director of Ghost Ranch suggested it might be due to the fact that it overlooks the dining/kitchen area of the ranch. Owned by the Presbyterian Church, Ghost Ranch is used by many organizations and groups as a setting for conferences and retreats. Staff are friendly and knowledgeable about the area. Next door to the office is a bookstore you may wish to browse in and a new museum is being installed as this book goes to press.

RATING: Easy, but with one rock scramble which may be difficult for some.

ROUND TRIP HIKING DISTANCE: About 5 miles.

APPROXIMATE HIKING TIME: 2.5 hours.

ALTITUDE RANGE: Highest point, 7077 feet; lowest point, 6500 feet; total vertical ascent, 600 feet.

SEASONAL CONSIDERATIONS: This trail can be hiked in all seasons; spring and fall would probably be the most pleasant; winter is OK if there has not been a recent heavy snowfall or rainstorm in the area. Summer hiking here will be hot.

ROUND TRIP DRIVING: 122 miles, approximately 2 hours and 40 minutes.

DRIVING DIRECTIONS: From the Santa Fe Plaza drive north on Washington Avenue, left on Paseo de Peralta, right on Old Taos Road to State Highway 84-285 continuing north to Española (approximately 23.5 miles, 45 minutes). Follow 84-285 green signs, turning left at the traffic light, crossing the Rio Grande bridge and continuing north on 84 through the village of Abiquiu. When you come to the Abiquiu Dam turnoff (Hwy #96, which you do not take), note your odometer reading. Continue north on US 84 for 6.3 miles where you will see a wooden sign for Ghost Ranch on the right hand side of the highway. Turn here. (You do not go as far as the Ghost Ranch Living Museum which is still 2 miles further up the highway.) At 1.1 miles this dirt road forks. Go to the left here and stop at the Ghost Ranch Office to let them know you're hiking. Drive back to the fork, turn left, and follow the road past the sign for the Dining Hall and Teepee Village. Follow the sign which says "Teepee Village" and "Trails to Kitchen Mesa and Box Canyon." At 1.9 miles you reach a parking area and a sign which says "No vehicles allowed beyond this point." Park here.

HIKING INSTRUCTIONS: Follow the dirt road a few yards further down a short hill and you will see a brown sign on the right which says "Kitchen Mesa." Follow the trail down the bank and across a small stream, through a small grove of trees and up the far bank. Straight ahead you will see your destination - the top of the high cliff. You will start to see blue-painted coffee cans nailed upside down on wooden posts; these markers continue the whole length of the trail, thus making it quite simple to find your way. The trail follows the river bank a short distance, then joins an old dirt road going up the hill to the right, and follows it through the rich Chinle formation soils of the valley floor. After 5 to 10 minutes of walking, the trail takes you up and over a low, but rather steep ridge. Watch your footing on the loose, gravelly soils. At the top you will be able to see the small box canyon stretching southeast, to your right, which the trail will follow, ascending by degrees to the mesa top at the far end.

After meandering along the base of some wonderfully sculptured Entrada sandstone cliffs, the trail crosses an arroyo, and starts going up the rocky talus slope of the canyon wall. Since the trail is steep from here to the top, proceed slowly, and watch your footing on the gravelly slope. When muddy, this section can be quite difficult to traverse. There are several dead-end paths branching off of the main trail in this section, so keep your eye out for the blue coffee cans and blue arrows painted on the rocks which delineate the actual trail. Just before you reach the top you will need to scramble up a narrow passage between huge boulders. There are adequate foot and hand holds if you look around for them; however, you will need to hoist a small child or your dog up the steepest section, and some adults may want help from their hiking companions.

It may not be possible to get very heavy
dogs up this vertical rock; the author was
unable to hoist her 125 pound Rottweiler up
here, even with the help of a friend. Some
find the ascent more difficult than the
return, and some dislike the descent, because they feel more exposed; in any case,
expect to proceed very slowly, and always
with great care, through this rocky section.

After the scramble the trail veers right,
crosses an arroyo, and goes steeply up on
easily ascended sandstone ledges to the top
of the ridge. Watch for blue arrows painted
on the rocks. You will probably have been
walking about an hour at this point. The
trail slowly bends to the right and follows
along the top of the mesa to the chalky
white, lunar landscape at its end. This
porous, hollow-sounding substance is called
the Todilto Formation and is gypsum, de-
posited by a lake that evaporated millions
of years ago. Roam around this point, and
enjoy the magnificent views, but don't get
too close to the edge since the gypsum is
crumbly, and the cliffs below it are sheer
and steep.

Walk back a few hundred yards to the beginning of the vegetation, find a comfortable
rock outcropping under a wind-sculpted
juniper, take out your picnic lunch, and
feast your senses. All is silence, sky, and
magnificent rock formations. Ghost Ranch,
surrounded by its green fields, sits right
under the cliffs; Cerro Pedernal (see page
173 for the Cerro Pedernal hike) is the
prominent flat-topped peak on the southern
horizon; the shadowy blue mesa to the northwest is Los Viejos; the multi-colored bluffs
all around you expose geologic history from
the reddish purple Chinle Formation muds at
the base to the tree-topped Dakota sandstone

at the top. At your feet may be patches of soil containing cryptogamic plants (lichens, fungi, etc.). Try not to step on them. The destruction of the cryptogams by walking or trampling has been determined to be the most significant factor in the erosion of desert soils. There may also be the grey-green leaves and small white trumpet-shaped flowers of Bigelow's sand abronia, or tufted sand verbena as it is sometimes called, a rare plant which grows only on Todilto gypsum soils.

The return to your car is down along the same trail by which you ascended. Enjoy the rich hues of the twisted juniper stumps as you return along the ridge, and when descending the trail back down the canyon, look for a few stately Douglas firs nestled in the coolest, shadiest nooks of the rocky walls.

(Note: If you want to spend more time hiking in the area you can take the short trail to Box Canyon, which starts in the same parking area. Follow along the streambed to a picturesque box canyon with steep walls, whose subdued lighting reminds one of a mysterious grotto. Ghost Ranch also provides a written description, available at the office for 25 cents, of the Chimney Rock Trail, just north of the Ranch, with much useful geological information.

North of Ghost Ranch on the paved highway is the Ghost Ranch Living Musuem. Run by the Forest Service, this museum, with its many wild animal exhibits and descriptions of the area, is also worth a visit.)

Cerro Pedernal

1 mile

Cerro Pedernal

15 foot vertical rock face

N

Jeep trail

Youngsville 5 miles

Forest Rd. 160

Temolime Canyon

□ Parking

CERRO PEDERNAL

by
John Muchmore and Norbert Sperlich

U.S. GEOLOGICAL SURVEY MAPS REQUIRED:
Youngsville and Cañones - 7.5 minute series.

SALIENT FEATURES: Cerro Pedernal is a landmark well known throughout north central New
Mexico. Its truncated pyramid shape is
visible from Taos to Cuba and from Chama to
Española. The mountain has appeared in
works of art by the very famous and the less
well-known artists of America. From its
summit, you will enjoy sweeping views in all
directions.

Cerro Pedernal is Spanish for "Flint Mountain." Flint (a variety of quartz) can be
found on the lower slopes of the mountain at
about 8,500 feet. For more than 10,000
years, Indians have used the flint from
Cerro Pedernal to make arrowheads and tools.

Much of the hike is on unmarked jeep trails,
the last part is steep and trail-less. This
hike is not suitable for inexperienced
hikers and not recommended for solo hiking.
While hiking on the jeep trails, make sure
that you don't miss a turnoff. Topo maps
and compass are essential for orientation,
in case you lose your bearing. The last
part of the hike is steep and rocky, re-
quiring sturdy boots with good traction.
This is dry country. Carry sufficient water
and be prepared for wind, cold, and rain.

RATING: Moderate in miles, strenuous because of the steep climbs.

ROUND TRIP HIKING DISTANCE: Approximately 9 miles.

APPROXIMATE HIKING TIME: 6 to 7 hours including ample time for stops.

ALTITUDE RANGE: Highest point, 9,862 feet; lowest point, 8,000 feet; total vertical ascent, 1,862 feet.

SEASONAL CONSIDERATIONS: Not safe when snow hides the jeep trails. The best time to visit is in the spring, fall, and early winter. A favorite area for elk and deer hunters.

ROUND TRIP DRIVING: 146 miles - approximately 3.5 hours.

DRIVING DIRECTIONS: Take Route 84/285 northbound from Santa Fe to Española. At the first traffic light in Española turn left and cross the Rio Grande. At the next light, turn right and continue on Route 84/285. Get into the left lane as you approach the third light. Turn left, still on Route 84/285. Stay on Route 84 (straight ahead) where Routes 84 and 285 separate about 6 miles north of Española. Continue north through the village of Abiquiu until you reach the Abiquiu Dam turnoff. There, turn left on Highway 96. Take your mileage at this intersection. Continue approximately 11 miles to the outskirts of Youngsville. As you approach a "Youngsville" sign, look for a gravel road that comes in on your left. This is Forest Road 100 (Rito Encino Road). In October 1989, this road was not marked at the turnoff. Turn left onto the gravel road and follow this road for about 5.5 miles, until you see a dirt road branch off to the left. Turn left onto this road and park your car in the meadow immediately after the turnoff. You are now on Forest Road 160, the Temolime Canyon jeep road. In October 1989, this road was not marked at the turnoff. However, a sign "160" appears some 150 yards along the road. The Temolime Canyon road is on the Youngsville and Cañones topo maps.

HIKING INSTRUCTIONS: Follow Forest Road 160 up Temolime Canyon for about 1 mile (20 minutes or more) to a fork in the road. Forest Road 160 continues straight ahead, but you take the jeep road that goes to the left (north). (This road appears on the topo maps as a broken line. On the Cañones map, look for the second "m" in the word "Temolime." That is where the road starts.) Ignore an abandoned logging road that branches right. In a few minutes, you will cross a drainage where the road turns to the left and starts climbing. Soon, the road turns to the right (north) again, and it appears to head toward the eastern end of the Pedernal summit ridge. Some 5 minutes after crossing the drainage, you may notice a block of flint to your right, with a "2" spray-painted on it. All around, and especially to the left of the road, are pieces of flint on the ground. In a few more minutes, you will come to a fork in the road. The road straight ahead (not shown on the topo map) appears to go toward the summit, but you take the road that goes off to the LEFT, in a westerly direction. Look at your watch. About 15 minutes after taking the left fork, as you are going uphill, you will notice a drainage on your left, where Gambel Oaks are growing. Just before your road is about to cross the drainage and make a turn to the left, look to your right. A road

comes in sharply from the right, and there
should be a cairn marking this intersection.

Take the road that comes in from the right.
It is not on the Youngsville topo map, but
its approximate location is shown on the
sketch map. At first, you will climb
steeply in an easterly direction. Then the
road turns north, toward the summit ridge.
It crosses a drainage and starts climbing
again, turning to the left and away from the
summit. This is obviously not the shortest
way to get to the top! After briefly
heading south, the road turns to the right
and takes you to almost level ground. In a
few minutes, you will come to the first of a
series of meadows. From the last intersection you have now hiked some 25 minutes
or more. For a while, the road heads toward
the center of the summit ridge, then turns
left and runs parallel to the ridge. Foiled
again! In the meadows, the car tracks may
not be highly visible. Mark dubious spots
for your return trip! It is easier getting
lost on the way down! Follow the car tracks
past the western end of the summit ridge to
a level spot between two pine trees. You
have now hiked some 40 minutes or more since
the last intersection. Ahead of you, the
terrain starts to descend, opening up splendid vistas over valleys, mesas, and mountain
ranges. Take a break and enjoy the views.

It will take another hour or so of strenuous
hiking to reach the summit. Look to your
right. A talus slope, studded with scrub
oak and piñon, rises up to the end of the
basalt ridge that forms the summit. There
is no trail here. Head up toward the narrow
end of the ridge, avoiding scrub oaks and
loose rocks as best you can. When you reach
the vertical basalt cliffs, go to the right
and follow a faint trail that runs along the

base of the cliffs. After about 150 yards (some 10 minutes of hiking) the trail passes between the cliff wall on the left and a large juniper tree on the right. (If you come to a cave in the rocks on your left, you have gone too far. Go back and look for the juniper tree.) Follow the trail some 10 yards past the juniper tree. Stop and look. To the right of the trail, there might be a cairn, and to your left, leaning against the rock wall, might be a log pole. The cliff on your left is somewhat broken up, providing hand and foot holds. This is the place to climb up, or to call it a day if it looks too scary to you. The first 15 feet are nearly vertical, but then you will come to a rough trail that goes up to your right, leading to the top of the ridge. Watch for loose rocks! When you come to the flat top, look for cairns. They will tell you where to start your descent on the way back. Any other way down is dangerous. Continue left on the ridge to its western end. This is the highest point of Pedernal. After you have enjoyed the views, you might want to go to the other end of the ridge, where the views are toward the east. Then find the cairn that marks the descent, and start your way down to the base of the cliffs. Once there, you will be tempted to head straight down to the jeep trail in the meadow below. However, to stay out of harm's way (loose rocks on a very steep slope) return to the meadow the same way you came up. Find the jeep road and retrace your route back to your car.

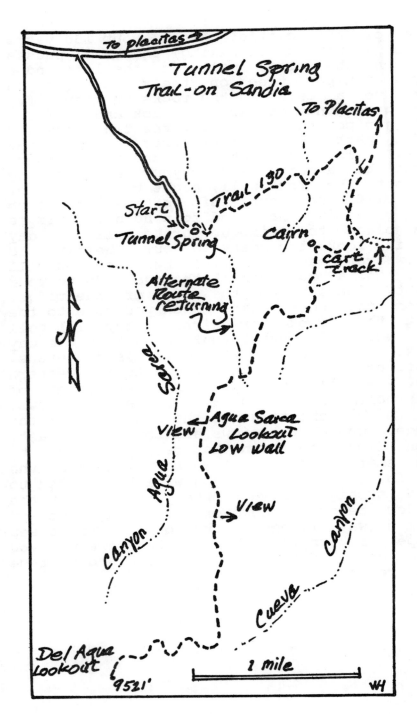

Tunnel Spring
Trail-on Sandia

To placitas →

To Placitas

Trail 130

Start
Tunnel Spring

Cairn

cart track

Alternate
Route
returning

Agua Sarca

N

Agua Sarca
Lookout
Low wall

VIEW

VIEW

Canyon

Cueva   Canyon

Del Aqua
Lookout
9521'

1 mile

WH

TUNNEL SPRING TRAIL TO DEL AGUA OVERLOOK
(In the Sandia Mountains)

by
Polly Robertson

U.S. GEOLOGICAL SURVEY MAP REQUIRED: Placitas - 7.5 minute series. The trail from Tunnel Spring east to its junction with the trail from Placitas is not shown on this map, and parts of the remainder of the trail have been changed since the map was issued.

SALIENT FEATURES: A hike offering sweeping views. No water. Lovely wildflowers. The walk from Tunnel Spring is all uphill on the north slope of Sandia; but it's ALL downhill returning.

RATING: Strenuous.

ROUND TRIP HIKING DISTANCE: 16 miles, but can be cut to any length one wishes, as it is an "out and back" hike. If one takes the alternate route down the arroyo returning, it is 13.5 miles.

APPROXIMATE HIKING TIME: 8 to 10 hours, plus time for stops.

ALTITUDE RANGE: Highest point, 9521 feet; lowest point, 6400 feet; total vertical ascent, 3100 feet.

SEASONAL CONSIDERATIONS: Unless you're sure of yourself, this hike should be taken when there is no snow on Sandia. It will be rather hot in midsummer.

ROUND TRIP DRIVING: 109 miles - about 2.5 hours.

DRIVING DIRECTIONS: Take I-25 south toward Albuquerque. After about 47 miles take Exit 242 towards Placitas. Make note of your odometer reading at the highway and go exactly 4.9 miles toward Placitas. Look for a dirt road to your right with a group of mail and newspaper boxes. There is a small sign (FR 231), as well as a prominent blond rock. Turn right here for 1.5 miles past several houses, bearing left if in doubt. The road is bumpy but passable. Watch out for a bump at the cattle guard. You will pass the spring on your right gushing through a pipe behind a stone wall. The parking area is immediately beyond.

HIKING INSTRUCTIONS: Trail #130 (North Crest Trail), on your right as you enter the parking area, is marked by three signs. Crest Trail signs show Agua Sarca 5 miles, Del Agua 8 miles and Sandia Crest 11 miles. You will start at 6400 feet. Agua Sarca Lookout is at about 7800 feet and Del Agua Lookout at 9521 feet. The time given on the sign to reach these spots is probably exaggerated for most Sierra Club hikers. Trail #130 ultimately reaches Sandia Crest after 11 miles. Any part of this distance is a lovely walk.

About 50 feet after entering the trail, you will come to a fork. Take the left fork past another set of signs admonishing the hiker about water, fire, etc . (If you wish to take the alternate return via the arroyo you will come out on the right hand trail.) The trail is a long roller-coasting traverse going east for about 1 mile, then it bears due south up Arroyo Colorado. Continue on this obvious trail (#130). At one point where the trail parallels an old cart track, be sure to bear right. Whenever you encounter what appears to be an old cart road, avoid it and remain on the narrow trail. Farther on, there is a row of stones on the right side of the trail. Keep straight ahead here, though there seems to be a cart track crossing the trail. Other than these two spots the trail is reasonably clear.

(Note: At about 3 1/2 miles from the start of this hike, the trail makes a sharp turn right, around the head of an arroyo. Just before this turn a trail drops down to the right into the arroyo. This is the start of a shorter return route down the arroyo which will save you 2 1/2 miles. Note this junction since you may want to return on it and it may be difficult to find on the way down.)

Continue on up the trail past the Agua Sarca overlook where there is a low stone wall on the right and expansive views to the west. At 8 miles from the start you will reach the Del Agua overlook, the turn-around point. Take time to enjoy the magnificent views to the west.

You may return to your car by the same route or take the shorter route previously mentioned. This shortcut is a bit of a scramble and rough in spots with large boulders. Caution should be exercised, and under NO circumstances should this arroyo trail be taken if it is raining, because of possible flash flooding. It will, however, cut off about 2.5 miles.

GLOSSARY

by Bill Chudd

Arroyo - A usually dry gully, at times containing a stream. After a rainstorm, or when there is a storm in nearby mountains, a dry arroyo may suddenly become a raging waterway.

Basalt - A dark igneous rock of volcanic origin, sometimes black and columnar.

Blaze - A mark on a tree made by chopping off a piece of bark. Blazes marking trails in the Santa Fe area generally consist of a short cut, with a longer cut below.

Blowhole - A hole through which gas or air can escape. Several deep pits in the Santa Fe area are commonly called blowholes, although they may or may not be the remains of ancient volcanic gas vents.

Borrego - A young lamb.

Cairn - A heap of stones; specifically, a pile of stones placed as a landmark, or to indicate a specific site or trail.

Caja del Rio - Box of the river. The Caja del Rio Canyon, popularly called Diablo Canyon, is a narrow, but not a box canyon.

Caldera - A large volcanic crater.

Camino - Road.

Cañada - Canyon, ravine.

Cerro - Hill.

Cholla - A tall spiny branching cactus with cylindrical stems.

Diablo Canyon - Devil Canyon (see Caja del Rio).

Divide - A ridge between two drainage areas.

Draw - A basin or ravine through which water drains.

Flume - An artificial channel, such as an inclined chute or trough, through which water is carried for irrigation or other purposes.

Frijoles - Beans (One of the crops culti-vated by the ancient Indians in Frijoles Canyon).

Moki stairway - Hand and toe holes dug by ancient Indians for scaling cliffs.

Petroglyph - A design cut or chipped into a rock face. Many interesting old Indian petroglyphs may be seen in the Santa Fe area.

Piñon - The pinyon pine tree.

Puerto Nambé - Nambé mountain pass.

Rio - River.

Rito - A small stream.

Scat - Excrement, animal droppings.

Scramble - To climb or descend using hands as well as feet.

Scree - Same as talus.

Saddle - A ridge between two peaks. Sometimes used loosely for any point where a trail or road tops a ridge.

Sangre de Cristo - Blood of Christ. The local mountain range was so named for the red color it reflects during some sunsets.

Santa Fe - Holy Faith. The full name of the city is "La Villa Real de la Santa Fe de San Francisco de Asis" - The Royal Village of the Holy Faith of St. Francis of Assisi.

Talus - A sloping bank of rocks at the base of a cliff.

Tarn - A high mountain lake or pond.

Tetilla - A small teat. Tetilla Peak was a landmark on the old Royal Road from Mexico, signaling the final approach to Santa Fe.

Tuff - A porous volcanic rock formed from compacted ash.

Viga - An exposed roof beam. (Originally a beam with which grapes or olives were pressed.)

Yucca - A plant of the lily family with sharply pointed, sword-shaped leaves.

SUGGESTED READING

Hiking

Evans, Harry. 50 Hikes in New Mexico. Pico Rivera, Cal.: Gem Guides Book Company, 1988.

Hill, Mike, ed. Hikers and Climbers Guide to the Sandia Mountains. Albuquerque: University of New Mexico Press, 1983.

Hoard, Dorothy. A Guide to Bandelier National Monument. Rev. ed. Los Alamos: Los Alamos Historical Society, 1989.

Hoard, Dorothy. Los Alamos Outdoors. Los Alamos: Los Alamos Historical Society, 1981.

Matthews, Kay. Hiking Trails of the Sandia and Manzano Mountains. Albuquerque: Heritage Associate, 1984.

Montgomery, Arthur, and Sutherland, Patrick K. Trail Guide to Geology of the Upper Pecos. Scenic Trips to the Geologic Past, No. 6. Socorro: New Mexico Bureau of Mines & Mineral Resources, 1975.

Overhage, Carl. Pecos Wilderness Trails for Day Walkers. Santa Fe: William Gannon, 1984.

Overhage, Carl. Six One-Day Walks in the Pecos Wilderness. Rev. ed. Santa Fe: The Sunstone Press, 1984.

Pettitt, Roland A. Exploring the Jemez Country. Los Alamos: Pajarito Publications, 1975.

Southwest Natural & Cultural Heritage Association. Pecos Wilderness. Recreation Opportunity Guide. Central Section. Albuquerque. (Available at the Santa Fe National Forest Office, Piñon Building, 1220 St. Francis Drive, Santa Fe, NM.)

Southwest Natural & Cultural Heritage Association. Pecos Wilderness. Recreation Opportunity Guide. Western and Northern Sections. Albuquerque. (Available at the Santa Fe National Forest Office, Piñon Building, 1220 St. Francis Drive, Santa Fe, NM.)

Ungnade, Herbert E. Guide to the New Mexico Mountains. Albuquerque: University of New Mexico Press, 1972.

Birds

Peterson, Roger Tory. A Field Guide to Western Birds. The Peterson Field Guide Series. Boston: Houghton Mifflin Co., 1961.

Robbins, Chandler S., et al. Birds of North America: A Guide to Field Identification. New York: Golden Press, 1983.

Scott, Shirley L., ed. Field Guide to the Birds of North America. 2d ed. Washington, D.C.: National Geographic Society, 1987. (Avaliable only in non-profit book stores. Try the Randall Davey Audubon Center in Santa Fe.)

Udvardy, Miklos D. F. The Audubon Society
Field Guide to North American Birds, Western
Region. New York: Alfred A. Knopf, 1977.

Geology

Baldwin, Brewster, and Kottlowski, Frank E.
Santa Fe. Scenic Trips to the Geologic
Past, No. 1. Socorro: New Mexico Bureau of
Mines and Mineral Resources, 1968.

Kues, Barry S. Fossils of New Mexico. New
Mexico Natural History Series. Albuquerque: University of New Mexico Press, 1982.

Muehlberger, W.R., and Muehlberger, Sally.
Española - Chama - Taos. A Climb Through
Time. Scenic Trips to the Geologic Past,
No. 13. Socorro: New Mexico Bureau of
Mines & Mineral Resources, 1982.

Thompson, Ida. The Audubon Society Field
Guide to North American Fossils. New York:
Alfred A. Knopf, 1982.

Mammals

Cockrum, E. Lendell. Mammals of the
Southwest. Tucson: The University of
Arizona Press, 1982.

Findley, James S. The Natural History of
New Mexican Mammals. New Mexico Natural
History Series. Albuquerque: University of
New Mexico Press, 1987.

Murie, Olaus J. A Field Guide to Animal
Tracks. The Peterson Field Guide Series.
Boston: Houghton Mifflin Co., 1974.

Mushrooms

Lincoff, Gary H. The Audubon Society Field Guide to North American Mushrooms. New York: Alfred A. Knopf, 1981.

Smith, Alexander H. A Field Guide to Western Mushrooms. Ann Arbor: The University of Michigan Press, 1975.

Trees and Shrubs

Elmore, Francis H., and Janish, Jeanne R. Shrubs and Trees of the Southwest Uplands. Popular Series, No. 19. Tucson: Southwest Parks & Monuments Association, 1976.

Lamb, Samuel H. Woody Plants of the Southwest. Santa Fe: The Sunstone Press, 1989.

Little, Elbert L. The Audubon Society Field Guide to North American Trees. Western Region. New York: Alfred A. Knopf, 1988.

Wildflowers

Arnberger, Leslie P. Flowers of the Southwest Mountains. Rev. ed. Popular Series, No. 7. Globe, Arizona: Southwest Parks and Monuments Association, 1982.

Craighead, John J., et al. Rocky Mountain Wildflowers. The Peterson Field Guide Series. Boston: Houghton Mifflin Co., 1963.

Dodge, Natt N., and Janish, Jeanne R. Flowers of the Southwest Deserts. Popular Series, No. 4. Globe, Arizona: Southwest Parks & Monuments Association, 1985.

Foxx, Teralene S., and Hoard, Dorothy.
Flowers of the Southwest Forests and Woodlands. Los Alamos: Los Alamos Historical Society, 1984.

Ivey, Robert DeWitt. *Flowering Plants of New Mexico*. 2d ed. Albuquerque, 1986.

Martin, William C., and Hutchins, Charles R. *Fall Wildflowers of New Mexico*. The New Mexico Natural History Series. Albuquerque: University of New Mexico Press, 1988.

_____. *Spring Wildflowers of New Mexico*. The New Mexico Natural History Series. Albuquerque: University of New Mexico Press, 1984.

_____. *Summer Wildflowers of New Mexico*. The New Mexico Natural History Series. Albuquerque: University of New Mexico Press, 1986.

Niehaus, Theodore F., et al. *A Field Guide to Southwestern and Texas Wildflowers*. The Peterson Field Guide Series. Boston: Houghton Mifflin Co., 1984.

Patraw, Pauline M. *Flowers of the Southwest Mesas*. Popular Series, No. 5. Globe, Arizona: Southwest Parks & Monuments Association, 1977.

Spellenberg, Richard. *The Audubon Society Field Guide to North American Wildflowers. Western Region*. New York: Alfred A. Knopf, 1979.

Tierney, Gail D., and Hughes, Phyllis. *Roadside Plants of Northern New Mexico*. Santa Fe: The Lightning Tree, 1983.

Weber, William A. Rocky Mountain Flora.
Boulder: Colorado Associated University
Press, 1976.

Miscellaneous

Auerbach, Phil S. Medicine for the Outdoors. Boston: Little, Brown, and Co.,
1986.

Barker, Elliot S. Beatty's Cabin: Adven-
tures in the Pecos High Country. Santa Fe:
William Gannon, 1977.

Christiansen, Paige W., and Kottlowski,
Frank E. Mosaic of New Mexico Scenery,
Rocks and History. Scenic Trips to the
Geologic Past, No. 8. Socorro: New Mexico
Bureau of Mines & Mineral Resources, 1972.

DeBuys, William. Enchantment and
Exploitation. The Life and Hard Times of a
New Mexico Mountain Range. Albuquerque:
University of New Mexico Press, 1985.

Kjellstrom, Bjorn. Be Expert with Map and
Compass: The Complete "Orienteering"
Handbook. New York: Charles Scribner's
Sons, 1976.

Pearce, T. M., ed. New Mexico Place Names:
A Geographical Dictionary. Albuquerque:
University of New Mexico Press, 1965.

Whitney, Stephen. Western Forests. The
Audubon Society Nature Guides. New York:
Alfred A. Knopf, 1985. (A general nature
guide.)

Wilkerson, James A., ed. Medicine for Moun-
taineering. Seattle: The Mountaineers,
1985.

INDEX OF HIKES